Be A Crypto MILLIONAIRE

Pushpendra Singh

Published by :

Invincible Publication Pvt. Ltd.

Published by:

Invincible Publishers

201A, SAS Tower, Sector 38, Gurugram, Haryana – 122003

Phone: +91-124-4034247, +91 9599066061

Website : www.invinciblepublishers.com

Sales Office : - 4760-61/23, Basement, Pratap Street, Ansari Road,

Daryaganj, New Delhi - 110002

Phone: +91-11-40198405

Email: invinciblepublishers@gmail.com

ISBN : 978-93-58863-96-3

Book Name : Be A Crypto Millionaire

First Edition: July 2023

Disclaimer

This book is meant for educational purposes only and is not a substitute for professional, financial or legal advice. Bearing the individual differences, it is of utmost importance that before making any financial decisions one must conduct thorough research, seek professional guidance, and consider their individual circumstances. The authors and publishers do not and cannot guarantee the accuracy or timeliness of the information provided, and disclaim any liability for any loss or damage resulting from its use. Cryptocurrency markets are volatile, and past performance is not indicative of future results. Stated by governmental authorities, crypto products and NFTs are unregulated and can be highly risky. There may be no regulatory recourse for any loss from such transactions. Thus, by reading this book, you agree to proceed with caution and take responsibility for your own financial decisions.

My story- The crypto millionaire

My story started in a small village of Uttar Pradesh. A simple life with all the routine things, an ambition for a good degree, a family that took care of me and a dream of a good job. My family is a clubhouse of engineers, myself, my father, two siblings, all of us, engineers. My love for computers was an expression of the genetic predisposition towards engineering and technology. This was pretty much all about my life up until I moved to Delhi. My parents had shifted to Delhi for better opportunities wishing to make my life easier through this change. And after my graduation I shifted there as well. After a little search party, I was finally offered a job at a renowned IT firm in Delhi. This was a dream come true. I had a five day week job, with an amazing work culture and a lot of time to try out new things as well. This spare time was the first clue into the world of cryptos for me. With some good hours to spare, I started with a freelancing company of my own. So, I would pick some projects with reachable clientele, work hard and deliver the best I could. The quality of my work and referrals slowly attracted an international clientele. This was the time when I started getting the deserved money for my work. It was during one such project that a client of mine introduced me to a thing called BITCOIN. In return for the project work, I was offered a few bitcoins. This is an incident, in 2015, when cryptocurrency was not very well known in India. At first it all seemed like Latin to me, what is bitcoin, and how would a currency that has no physical form be used as a payment form. And where was this wallet? Who made this currency? Who regulated it? All these questions itched my general knowledge at first. However, she insisted on paying the amount through bitcoins, so I researched the topic, took some initial help from my client for the setup and then received a few bitcoins in my wallet. The only motive behind getting into the unknown with these new coins was to adapt to this new international clientele and their nature of demands. Even after a fair understanding of the set up, I drew some analogy between bank currencies and cryptocurrencies, taking their workings, storage to be the same. I saved the coins for a later use, being callous with the keys and the credentials. A Year passed and I forgot all about the Bitcoins but somehow a year later, these coins were all that people could talk about. I got to know through news that Bitcoins had soured in prices and the term was now a lay man parlance. My search for their digital footprints began, I tried really hard to find those keys that my client had sent to me a year back. All the searches yielded no result and it was heartbreaking to know that I had lost the keys to my treasure trove. I tried everything from account recovery, to email redressals but unlike other currency systems, cryptocurrencies are decentralized with no mediators, leading to no possible way of key recovery. Till date just the reminder of it, sends chills down my spine. And somewhere the Bitcoins lay quietly hidden in my wallet. It was this lack of knowledge and ignorance that made me suffer a loss. If it hadn't been the case, I would have had sums of money that could have changed my life forever. Thus, hereon it became my mission to fuel awareness regarding technology in India. Bitcoin was a futuristic idea back then and most of us had no idea about it. On the contrary, things were integrating around block chain technology in other countries. This is the journey I savaged after my hard-learned lesson. Since then I have created 1000 plus videos on YouTube through my four different channels in addition to other social media platforms. These channels publish videos and content regarding block chain technology and cryptocurrency, making this knowledge easily adaptable to the common man in India. Gradually my work diversified to crypto-mining as well. I wanted to understand the bigger picture of the crypto world which led me to research and learn a lot about the topic. It is this passion, curiosity and hard work that helped me to build expertise, successful assets and investments with cryptos. Whether it is helping web3 startups to better their technology, or helping traders earn better through a self-made tool, smartviewai.com, or helping a common man learn better about these future technologies, my work revolves around an immense love for this technology. This is the reason why the knowledge series is finding expression through this book as well. It is a written note to those people who wish to learn, invest, trade or reinvent the world around cryptocurrency and blockchain technology.

About the author

Pushpendra Singh is a Microsoft certified software engineer, founder of SmartViewAi platform; a finance educator and a consultant. His expertise in technology is rooted in years of industrial exposure in software development. His work has made some of the finest software's for challenging projects like supply chain management, centralized finance system and cryptocurrency market. His years of expertise and experience, is of use for many people today, ranging from beginners to experts in the field. His ed-tech channel on YouTube, which discusses the topics of decentralized finance systems and web3 has grown to a monthly viewership of over a million. A tech enthusiast and an engineer at heart, Pushpendra dedicates his work to the mass adoption of technology worldwide. He is a visionary taking it to be his mission, to educate the young minds in India of the futuristic technologies and the advancements of the present. Though his forte lies with cryptocurrency and blockchain technology, his actions signify the bigger revolution that has set pace in the financial world of our times.

About the book

This book is for anyone who foresees the future through the eyes of an investor. In short, this book is for the investor of tomorrow. It is a strategic guide to building wealth with cryptocurrency and blockchain technology. It can be of use for anyone that wishes to begin, expand or revisit the understanding and use of cryptocurrency for his financial growth. The crypto millionaire challenges common notions around the volatility of cryptos and the juggernauts around its unpredictable behaviors, Pushpendra takes the reader to a deeper and a firmly rooted understanding of the technology and the currency at large. This book is to prepare the aspiring investor for a smart investment with cryptos, teaching caution and freedom; analysis and intuition; trends and maneuvering, crafted with his years of experience in the market.

Index

Chapter 1

Understanding Crypto Market

The working of cryptocurrency is backed by blockchain technology. But before we even begin to understand about cryptocurrency and anything related to it, we must understand why there was a need for this invention and what stage of financial evolution it takes us to.

Cryptocurrency is a form of digital currency that is entirely digital in existence and is a collection of number sequences. It is protected by encryption of cryptography. Unlike traditional transaction methods, cryptocurrency works on a decentralized financial system of blockchain technology.

If we go back, the transactions system first started with a barter system, exchanging items for items. This system had its limitations as item values differed and trades became unbalanced. This led to the evolution of precious metal and metal coins. This form of money had intrinsic value and this validated its utility. Soon, when governments were forming across the globe and due to limitation of metal reserves, rising cases of theft, metal coins were replaced by currency notes. Here the validator was the trust in the stability and authority of the government. Currency notes, themselves don't have an intrinsic value but the word of the government makes it valuable. Currency notes served the human financial systems for quite some time but with the coming of the internet age currencies required a digital representation.

The money without being seen was fulfilling its purpose of facilitating transactions with banks keeping a record of each credit and debit.

With cryptocurrency, we are still operating by transferring digital assets from one person to another. However, in this system, instead of separate records with different banks and centralized authorities, one detailed ledger is maintained of all records. This ledger is available at all connected nodes of the blockchain network. So, let's say if you use 50 Bitcoins somewhere, the data verification will not happen with the respective bank but each node of the blockchain network will validate the transaction, eliminating the risk of fraudulent entries, manipulations or omissions. Blockchain technology creates open traceable transaction systems. But if everyone can see the transactions, wouldn't it be a violation of privacy? This is the reason why transactions are encrypted. These transactions are built into blocks each having its own HASH ID, that changes with each alteration and incorporates the previous block HASH ID as well. This connection makes it difficult for anyone to temper with transaction records.

Why did Cryptocurrency evolve?

As you know by now Cryptocurrency runs on the system of Blockchain technology, this technology evolved to solve the security and traceability challenges that run with the currency notes system.

As a solution, Crypto Blockchain has an elaborate ledger with millions of copies of the transactions. These transactions are automated and processed in fractions of seconds. Thus, this decentralized system makes international payments faster and cuts down on processing fees. Crypto transactions are also hundred percent traceable as tempering the millions of individual ledger copies is almost impossible as of now. Cryptos do not require banks to validate transactions, all it requires is an internet connection and system node connected to the blockchain network. And with penetration of the internet in our society, cryptocurrency offers a more streamlined system of transactions.

How can you earn money with cryptocurrency?

Cryptocurrency is a fairly new currency avenue. However, like any other asset, crypto offers many ways with which its users can make money. In my experience I discovered the following-:

1. **Crypto trading-** Crypto trading involves buying and selling the crypto currencies within a short span of time. Unlike investment, trading does not require you to hold investments for longer periods of time. Crypto trading should only be done after a rooted understanding of crypto volatility and market authenticity.

2. **Crypto investment-** This is the method of buying

and holding a cryptocurrency in the anticipation of its price appreciation in the long run. Investment starts with identifying the right coin that matches your investment goal, principal sum and it's behind the scenes workings.

3. **Mining-** Blockchain involves an elaborate ledger of transactions, which requires validation at each node of the network. This process is done by the miners that deploy their systems to work towards the same. Mining is a resource intensive activity and it requires a hardware setup to run.

4. **Staking-** Staking is a way to earn rewards in terms of cryptocurrency by employing the proof-of-stake method. In this method a miner stakes a few of his crypto holdings. By staking these coins, the miner contributes to the network's security and consensus mechanism, and in return earning additional cryptocurrency rewards.

5. **Masternodes-** Masternodes are special nodes in the blockchain network that work beyond the normal routine of the network nodes. Besides validating transactions, super nodes work to facilitate the blockchain network. They perform various tasks, such as processing transactions, facilitating advanced features, and enhancing the network's performance and security.

6. **Yield Farming and Liquidity Mining-** These are practices commonly associated with decentralized finance (DeFi) platforms. Yield farming involves lending or staking cryptocurrencies on DeFi platforms to earn interest or yield. Liquidity mining refers to providing

liquidity to decentralized exchanges or protocols and earning rewards in the form of tokens.

7. **Participating in Initial Coin Offerings (ICOs) or Token Sales-** ICOs or Token sales work somewhat like the Initial Public Offerings. These are initial sales done to raise funds by the blockchain projects. Once the values of these currencies appreciate, it can give a huge return to the investor.

8. **Providing Services-** Services can range from consultancy, education, freelancing, content creation to so many other options.

How is the crypto market different from traditional financial markets?

1. **Decentralization-** Cryptocurrencies and their markets are decentralized meaning there is no one centralized entity that is regulating the system. In traditional financial markets, centralized bodies like SEBI and RBI govern the majority of the rules of the transaction system. But in cryptocurrency there is no regulatory body to validate or keep things under check.

2. **Accessibility-** Cryptos are accessible to anyone who has an internet connection whereas traditional financial markets require intermediaries and authority stamps to trade. Cryptocurrency is borderless and globally accessible.

3. **Market Hours-** Cryptocurrency markets run 24*7 and are not affected by geography or time differences. Whereas traditional markets operate on a fixed hours and days model.

4. **Volatility-** Since cryptocurrencies are not governed by any central authority and its market size is still in its growth stage, cryptocurrencies are known for their volatile nature. In a matter of seconds their prices can drop down from highs to the minimal lows. Traditional assets do have volatility but there are governing forces that keep them under regulation.

5. **Market structure-** Cryptocurrency trading is often conducted on decentralized exchanges (DEXs) or centralized exchanges (CEXs) that operate differently from traditional stock exchanges. Additionally, the cryptocurrency market has a diverse range of cryptocurrencies with varying use cases, whereas traditional financial markets primarily deal with stocks, bonds, commodities, and other established financial instruments.

6. **Regulation-** Regulations around cryptocurrency vary from country to country. While there are some countries where everyday exchanges are being done using cryptocurrencies, however, there are some countries that refuse to even legalize the new form of currency.

7. **Information flow-** The availability and flow of information in the cryptocurrency market differ from traditional financial markets. Cryptocurrency markets are heavily influenced by social media, online communities, and news sources specific to the crypto industry. Traditional financial markets rely on established financial news outlets, research reports, and company disclosures for information dissemination.

8. **Market Size and Liquidity:** The cryptocurrency

market, while growing rapidly, is still relatively small compared to traditional financial markets. Traditional financial markets, such as the stock market, have much larger market sizes and higher liquidity due to the participation of institutional investors, large corporations, and extensive trading volumes.

Chapter 2

Analyzing Cryptocurrency

In definitional terms, Analysis is the systematic examination and study of a subject to gain a comprehensive understanding of its various components, characteristics, relationships, and underlying principles.

It entails the deconstruction of complex entities or situations into smaller elements and the subsequent evaluation of each part to extract insights, draw logical conclusions, and facilitate well-informed decision-making.

Thus, analyzing something is important to make a well-informed decision. This decision is a summary of detailed study of the widest possible aspects of the given matter. Analysis does not guarantee the selection of a right decision but it increases the chance of selecting the most suitable or profiting option. The same analysis is extremely important when it comes to cryptocurrency. As Reason makes it possible for us to understand the wilderness of our world and channelize it, similarly analysis helps us to make sense of what appears as randomness. It is analysis that helps the investor to ride through the volatility of the crypto market and cushion any negatives that can arise from here.

Before I begin to lay the foundations of crypto analysis, I would like to address one of the most common questions asked about cryptos.

Is cryptocurrency a good investment?

I always say this, cryptocurrency is a fairly new system and it is still in its nascent stages. This evolving nature of cryptocurrency will require constant experimentation and changes, thus it becomes a little tricky to plan out an investment with it. In my opinion, one should only invest the sum that they can afford to lose in crypto. I say this because a lot of factors are at play here including but not limited to government regulations, technological changes, frauds and hacks. Considering these events, I always advise one to not put their foot down with crypto rather take a smarter road of using cryptocurrency as a portfolio diversification tool. There have been people who made billions and millions with crypto but there are also some who lost everything with it. The only difference between the two is their degrees of understanding and smartness with the asset. This is why this book can be of help to every kind of reader. I do not push for a universal approach for everyone. I can provide you with knowledge, the know-how, strategies and tools but it is you who has to find out your own style.

Now let's start with the different types of cryptocurrency investing

Different Types of Cryptocurrency Investing

The general explanation for investing in cryptocurrency is buying and holding the coin for a relatively longer period in anticipation of a profit. However, investing is just not limited to this activity. Besides direct purchasing and holding, Crypto investment can also involve the following-:

- Invest in cryptocurrency companies: One can invest in companies that support the concept, vision, exchange and utility of cryptocurrency. These companies can include cryptocurrency mining companies, mining hardware makers. Some of the well known companies like BlockFi, Stellar Development Foundation and PayPal Holdings Inc. support cryptocurrency along with many others. You also can invest in companies like MicroStrategy Inc. (MSTR), which holds large amounts of cryptocurrency on their balance sheets.

- Invest in cryptocurrency-focused funds: Crypto-currency focused funds are like index funds, that group together individual funds to provide an investor with better portfolio holdings. These can prove to be highly useful for investors who wish to balance and diversify their holdings, manage risk and use expert advice in creating fund options. You have a choice of exchange-traded funds (ETFs), such as index funds and futures funds, in addition to a range of cryptocurrency investment trusts.

Some crypto-focused funds invest in cryptocurrency

directly, while others invest in crypto-focused companies or derivative securities such as futures contracts.

- Invest in a cryptocurrency Roth IRA: If you're interested in investing in cryptocurrency while enjoying the tax benefits associated with an individual retirement account (IRA), one option to explore is investing in a cryptocurrency Roth IRA. By utilizing the services of a crypto IRA provider, you can not only access potential tax advantages but also ensure secure storage for your cryptocurrency assets. This approach combines the potential growth of cryptocurrency investments with the long-term benefits and protections provided by a Roth IRA structure.
- Become a crypto miner or validator: Crypto miner and validators invest their time, efforts, resources and skills into the network and they are rewarded with cryptocurrency in return.

What are the types of cryptocurrency analysis?

There are several types of analysis that can be applied to cryptocurrencies:

1. Fundamental Analysis: Fundamental analysis involves analyzing the fundamentals of the cryptocurrency. This basically tells us about the story, and the intrinsic value of a cryptocurrency. Through this particular type of analysis one can understand its underlying technology, use case, team, partnerships, adoption, and market potential. This helps to understand and gauge relevancy, growth and the cryptocurrency's value over a longer term.

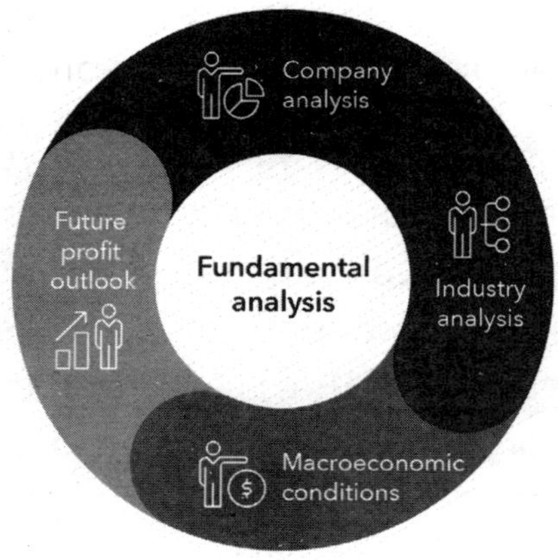

2. Technical Analysis: Technical analysis involves the examination of historical price and volume data, as well as the application of technical indicators and chart patterns, to identify trends and potential trading opportunities. This analysis involves studying price charts, trading volume, and market indicators to identify patterns, trends, and potential price movements. Under technical analysis, traders use historical price data, charts and mathematical tools to make predictions about future price movements.

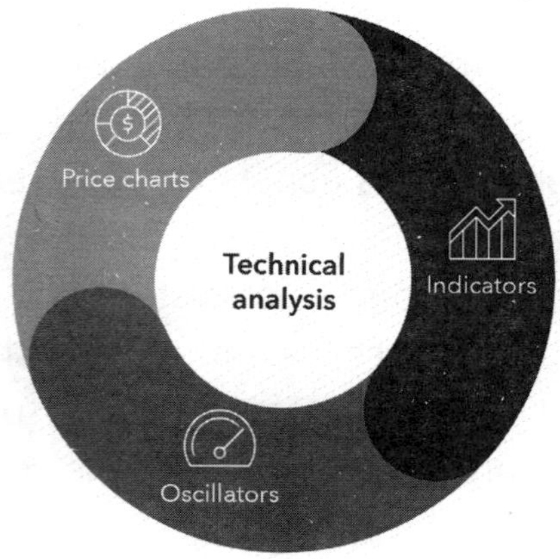

3. Sentiment Analysis: Sentiment refers to an opinion that is largely influenced by emotions thus sentiment analysis involves gauging investor emotions and market sentiment towards a cryptocurrency. It includes analyzing various channels of mass communications like social media discussions, news sentiment, and market sentiment indicators to understand the overall sentiment and potential impact on the price and market behavior of the cryptocurrency.

4. Quantitative Analysis: Quantitative analysis majorly involves statistical and mathematical tools for analysis. These tools and techniques are used to analyze large datasets related to cryptocurrencies. It includes analyzing historical price and trading volume data, as well as applying various statistical models to identify patterns, correlations, and potential trading opportunities.

5. Network Analysis: Network analysis focuses on the most important technological aspect of cryptocurrency which is its network. By studying the network dynamics of a cryptocurrency you can know a lot about the cryptocurrency, its team, level of seriousness of the project etc. The blockchain network is studied for its security, scalability, and overall health. It involves analyzing transaction volumes, network nodes, mining activity, and consensus mechanisms to gain insights into the cryptocurrency's network.

6. Risk Analysis: Risk analysis involves assessing the potential risks associated with investing in a particular cryptocurrency. It includes evaluating factors such as market volatility, regulatory risks, technological risks,

liquidity risks, and security risks. Understanding and managing these risks is crucial for making informed investment decisions.

7. Economic Analysis: Economic analysis examines the broader economic factors that can influence cryptocurrencies. It involves analyzing factors such as inflation, interest rates, geopolitical events, and government policies to assess their potential impact on the cryptocurrency market.

8. Comparative Analysis: Comparative analysis involves comparing and benchmarking different cryptocurrencies against each other. It includes evaluating different cryptocurrencies under markers such as market capitalization, trading volume, technology, adoption, and competitive advantages to assess their relative strengths and weaknesses.

Chapter 3

Fundamental Analysis

The technical analysis for a cryptocurrency is similar to the ones done for other financial assets. The same tools like pie charts, candlesticks etc are used in both cases. However, the same is not true for Fundamental analysis. Fundamental analysis is used by the investors that are looking for a long-term investment strategy. A crypto asset cannot be analyzed by using the traditional indicators and requires a different framework.

There are three factors that are important to Fundamentally analyze a cryptocurrency. These include-:

a. Financial metrics

b. On-chain metrics

c. Project metrics

a. **Financial metrics-** The financial metrics provide insights into various aspects of an organization's financial status, profitability, efficiency, and overall financial well-being. They are quantitative measurements that assess the financial performance and health of the given cryptocurrency project.

1. **Liquidity and trading volume-** The value of an asset is also dependent upon its liquidity. Liquidity refers to the ease with which an asset can be bought or sold without significantly impacting its price. For example if you buy a car and five years later you wish to sell it, the liquidity in this case is not so lucrative. Firstly the ease to sell is dependent upon many external factors and secondly it is a depreciating asset. On the contrary, gold is a liquid asset. It either appreciates or stabilizes in value and can be bought and sold easily. The same thing is to be checked while considering buying a crypto asset. High positive investor confidence as it allows for smoother transactions and price discovery. When a cryptocurrency has high liquidity, it means there is a large number of buyers and sellers in the market. Trading volume, on the other hand, represents the total number of shares or units of a cryptocurrency traded within a specific period. It indicates the level of market activity and interest in a particular cryptocurrency. Higher trading volumes generally suggest a more active and liquid market, providing traders with more opportunities to enter and exit positions.

2. Market cap- I consider Market cap as a very important marker, so, I 'll try to explain it with an example. Consider this, each family member owns a piece of land. These plots are of different sizes and thus of different values. The piece of land that belongs to your

mother is let's say 1500 sq. ft. and your plot size is 100 sq. ft. Now, the total land holdings of this family is 10,000 sq ft. Thus, your market cap will be 100 sq. ft., your mother's will be 1500 sq. ft. Market cap tells us about the relative size and value of a cryptocurrency within the overall market. Cryptocurrencies with higher market caps are generally considered to have a larger presence and more established position in the market.

3. Supply mechanism- Each cryptocurrency has a different supply mechanism. Some have a fixed supply like Bitcoin, some have an inflationary supply chain meaning new coins will be created over time, eg Ethereum. Cryptocurrencies with a limited supply may experience increased scarcity and potentially higher value over time, while those with an inflationary supply may face the challenge of maintaining value in the face of continuous coin or token creation. In an inflationary supply chain, rate of coin generation and previous activity should be studied. Under fixed supply mode, the number of coins that are generated and the remaining sum should be considered.

b. **On-chain metrics-** On-chain metrics are quantitative measurements that provide insights into the activities and behavior occurring on a blockchain network. These metrics analyze the data recorded on the blockchain itself and can help assess the network's usage, health, and user behavior.

Example

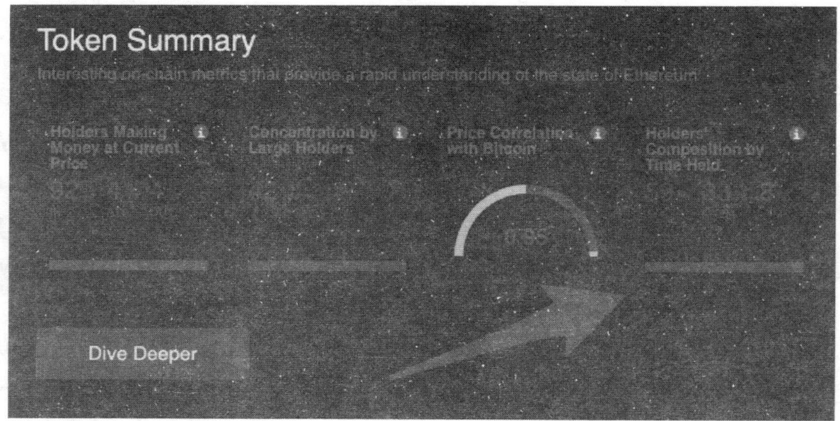

1. **Transaction value:** It is the value of the cryptocurrency involved in a particular transaction or set of transactions (no of transaction x value of a coin). Analyzing transaction value provides insight into the economic activity, trading volume, and overall health of a cryptocurrency network. However, transaction value alone cannot provide all important insights thus should be used along with additional factors such as transaction volume, frequency, fees, and the number of addresses involved to gain a comprehensive understanding of the network's transaction behavior. For instance, in the market, the transaction value of an item might be really high but its trade volume might be really less. That indicates an inflationary price, assessed more than the item's actual demand.

Assessing transaction value is critical to understanding liquidity, adoption, and economic activity within a cryptocurrency network. Higher transaction values indicate greater value transfers, the fact that many users are interested in it and are performing significant transactions within the network.

2. **Transaction count:** It is the count of the number of transactions that have been done over a period of time. Transaction count is often used as an important metric to evaluate the adoption, popularity, and growth of a cryptocurrency. An increasing transaction count over time suggests a growing user base, expanding network usage, and a thriving ecosystem.

3. **Active addresses:** Active addresses in cryptocurrency refer to the number of unique accounts or wallets that have participated in transactions within a specific cryptocurrency network during a specific period. Active addresses help us to judge the authenticity of the project as the more activity occurs on the network, it signals increasing interest of the users in the project.

When the number of active addresses is high, it indicates that more individuals or organizations are involved in transactions or other activities using the cryptocurrency.

Example:

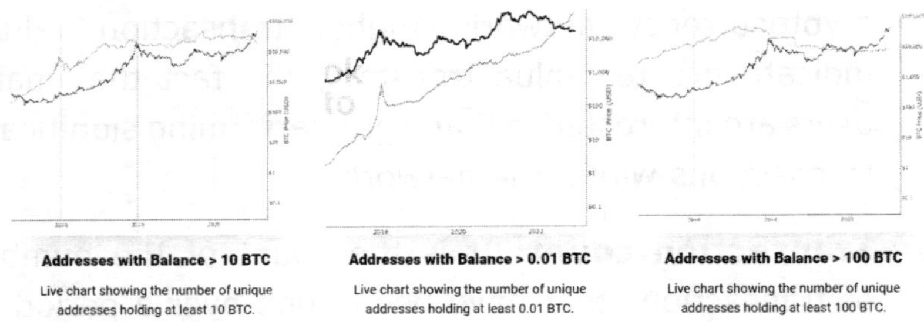

Addresses with Balance > 10 BTC

Live chart showing the number of unique addresses holding at least 10 BTC.

Addresses with Balance > 0.01 BTC

Live chart showing the number of unique addresses holding at least 0.01 BTC.

Addresses with Balance > 100 BTC

Live chart showing the number of unique addresses holding at least 100 BTC.

1. **Paid fee:** We will learn in the later chapters about mining and miners. Mining is an activity that is done to validate transactions on the network and it is done by miners. The purpose of paying a fee on transactions is to incentivize these network participants(miners) to prioritize and process transactions in a timely manner. The fee acts as a reward for the computational resources and efforts done by the miners to maintain network integrity and security. Analyzing the paid fee can provide insights into the demand for network resources and the cost associated with conducting transactions within the cryptocurrency network. Higher paid fees may indicate increased competition for transaction processing and can reflect the network's overall activity and usage. However the same should be corroborated with other metrics as well, in order to draw a complete picture.

2. Hash rate and amount staked: Higher the hash rate, higher is the interest of miners in the coin, and vice versa.

c. **Project metrics:** Project metrics are qualitative measurements used to assess the progress, performance, and success of a specific project. These metrics provide insights into various aspects of the project's development, execution, and achievement of objectives. They help project managers and stakeholders track key indicators to ensure the project is on track and meeting its goals.

1. **White paper:** a textual document that has an overview of the technology that is used in the cryptocurrency. This includes structure of the blockchain, use case, future road maps, goals, consensus mechanism, supply and distribution. Before investing in any cryptocurrency, it is always recommended to read the white paper to understand the cryptocurrency better.

2. **Tokenomics and Initial distribution-** Tokenomics refers to the study of the economic principles and mechanisms underlying a cryptocurrency or token. It involves analyzing factors such as the token's supply, distribution, utility, and governance within the associated blockchain network. Initial distribution, as part of tokenomics, focuses specifically on how tokens are initially allocated among participants. This process can impact factors like decentralization, concentration of ownership, and the fairness of distribution. Analyzing the initial distribution helps assess the potential impact on the token's value, network security, and the level of participation from various stakeholders. It helps us to understand if the percentage of holdings is evenly distributed or concentrated in few hands that can use the leverage to manipulate various metrics.

3. **The team-** By studying the team, investors and analysts can assess the team's qualifications, experience, and their ability to execute the project successfully. A strong team increases confidence in the project's potential, while a weak team may raise concerns about the project's viability, longevity and the team's capacity to deliver results. A skilled team with relevant experience in areas such as blockchain technology, finance, or software development is more likely to overcome challenges and deliver on their promises.

4. **Competitors-** Analyzing competitors allows investors to compare and evaluate different investment opportunities and different metrics within the cryptocurrency market. They can assess factors such as the potential of the team, nature of technology, external partnerships, and community engagement to determine which projects have a higher likelihood of success and align with their investment goals.

Chapter 4:

Technical analysis

What is technical analysis?

Technical analysis is a type of analysis that uses past price actions to predict trends of the future. Unlike fundamental analysis that brings into consideration various other aspects around cryptocurrency, technical analysis strictly focuses on price action and trading volume. This analysis is also known as charting.

Technical analysis requires indicators to study price movements. Trading indicators are mathematical calculations, which are plotted as lines on a price chart and can help traders identify certain signals and trends within the market. There are two types of trading indicators, lagging and leading. The former studies past movements and indicates momentum. It helps us to build trends and patterns. On the contrary, A leading indicator is a forecast signal that predicts future price movements.

Why is technical analysis used?

Fundamental analysis is useful to build a larger and a broader understanding of a project. It helps to understand and judge the authenticity, vision and genuinity of a cryptocurrency model. However, fundamental analysis is more useful to build a foundation but it is not so useful for short term trading, this is where technical analysis comes into picture. As discussed above it is customizable and can be performed on various time periods. When you wish to buy an asset, the first thing you do is check its current price. E.g. you are in for buying a cryptocurrency, let's say ripple and you check its current price which is at 34 INR. You can't make a decision of either buying or selling because you don't know the comparative prices from different time periods, the similar case being with trading volume. In this case technical analysis is performed, to understand the price action and trading volume over different time frames. This helps the trader to make a more informed trading decision. Trading indicators are mathematical calculations, which are plotted as lines on a price chart and can help traders identify certain signals and trends within the market. Indicators play a central role in technical analysis. Indicators are mathematical calculations performed on a wide range of data of price action and trading volume which is used to analyze market conditions, identify trends, generate signals, and assess the strength of price movements. It is important to note that any indicator including moving average should only be used to confirm the established observations that you build after studying price action. Indicators are used to confirm what is already established through studying trends. They by themselves cannot and should not be used for buying, selling or holding assets.

Although there are many indicators in the study sphere, for most of the trading and investment activities you only need these four basic indicators. As you gradually become experts at using these, you can study other indicators as well.

But before moving forward let me explain few terms that we are going to use to explain the application of these indicators:

1. Bullish trend-In the context of cryptocurrency, a bullish trend refers to a positive and upward price movement in the market. It implies an optimistic overall sentiment and market conditions, with an increasing demand for cryptocurrencies reflected in the rising trade volumes and prices. During a bullish trend, prices generally rise, with investors and traders investing their money in anticipation of further rise in prices and profits.

Several factors can contribute to a bullish trend in the cryptocurrency market:

1. Positive news and developments: If there is positive news through the government or in international arenas, it can drive higher prices and volumes for the cryptocurrency. Regulatory clarity, partnerships, technological advancements, or increased adoption of cryptocurrencies can drive positive sentiment among investors and fuel a bullish trend.

2. Increased investor interest: As more people become interested in the activity around a cryptocurrency project, the more its prices tend to rise. Increased investor interest fuels demand and indirectly through money fuels supply as well. This increased interest

can come from retail investors, institutional investors, or even governments.

3. Market cycles and momentum: Cryptocurrency markets often experience cycles of bull and bear trends. After a prolonged bearish period, a shift in market sentiment can create a bullish trend. Positive price momentum and the fear of missing out (FOMO) can attract more investors and contribute to the upward movement.

4. Bearish trend-A bearish trend in cryptocurrency refers to a downward price movement and negative sentiment in the market. Bearish trend represents pessimism in the investors and traders and signals that there is a demand-supply discrepancy. During a bearish trend, prices generally decline, and investors and traders may anticipate further price drops.

Several factors can contribute to a bearish trend in the cryptocurrency market:

1. Negative news and events: Unfavorable news such as regulatory restrictions, security breaches, hacking incidents, or negative market sentiment can tur around a positive investor confidence into negative and contribute to a bearish trend.

2. Market corrections: Market corrections can follow after a pump-dum cycle or after a prolonged high in prices. It can also occur to correct volume and price mismatches. This can be driven by profit-taking, overvaluation concerns, or a need for consolidation after rapid price gains.

3. Economic factors: Every asset and its value in the

market is impact by external factors like geopolitics, economic activities etc. However these factors impact cryptocurrencies with more brutality than other assets, as cryptocurrency do not run under a single centralized authority. Negative economic factors can trigger a bearish trend as investors seek safe investment options. A positive economic factor can drive more money into this investment avenue as people have more money to spend generally at this time.

4. Regulatory actions: Government regulations and policies regarding cryptocurrencies can have a significant impact on market sentiment. If regulators introduce restrictive measures or uncertainty regarding the legal framework, it can create a bearish trend.

1. Sideways market -

A sideways market, also known as a horizontal or ranging market, refers to a period in which the price of an asset, including cryptocurrencies, moves for a stretched period of time within a relatively tight trading range, between its support and resistance without any clear upward or downward trend. Sideways market is the opposite of the trending market as the price keeps moving between the support and resistance bands but does not make any significant movement in either direction.

Contrary to the general belief money can be made during a sideways market as well. A trader can benefit from the price movements that bounce back and forth between the upper and lower boundaries of the range. This can create trading opportunities for individuals who employ range-bound strategies, such as buying at support levels and selling at resistance levels.

Several factors can contribute to a sideways market in the cryptocurrency space:

1. **Market indecision:** Lack of conviction and clarity of the future of a crypto asset can result in a safe trading sentiment in the market.

2. **Balance of supply and demand:** When the supply and demand of a crypto asset becomes balanced it can lead to a lack of momentum and a sideways movement. A balanced volume sustains a balanced price.

3. **Consolidation after a trend:** A sideways market can occur after a significant price trend, whether it's bullish or bearish. This consolidation phase allows the market

to find equilibrium and reassess the next direction.

4. **Lack of significant news or events:** Without major news or events that drive the market in a particular direction, the price may stay range-bound until new information or catalysts emerge.

Top 4 indicators for technical analysis

1. Moving average-: Moving average indicator, is an average of the price movement over a selected period of time. It helps us to identify trends and smooth out price fluctuations over a specified period of time. Moving average is a customizable tool, you can configure timelines, no. of comparative time lines and plot trends with them. Traders can choose different time periods depending on their trading strategy and the cryptocurrency they are analyzing. Shorter-term moving averages, such as 20-day or 50-day moving averages, are often used for short-term trading, while longer-term moving averages, such as 100-day or 200-day moving averages, are used for longer-term analysis.

A particular type of moving average, Exponential Moving average is considered a valuable indicator by traders. Exponential moving average (EMA), places more weight on recent price data compared to older data. It uses a formula that incorporates a smoothing factor, giving more significance to recent prices. Traders often prefer EMAs when they want to react more quickly to price changes.

Why use Moving Average?

The answer to this lies in the question of why we use averages in general. Try to understand this using this example. Let's talk about a vast encyclopedia that has elaborated on various subjects and has rich information. It is a lengthy text with so much information in it. But what if each chapter came with a summary at the end? Wouldn't it make so much difference and give your brain an easier way to understand, recap and remember things. Averages, just like these textual summaries, ease out the vast data and number fluctuations, giving us coherence and a consolidated picture of everything. Similarly, moving averages in the crypto's case, does the same: it smooths the price fluctuations and the moving fluctuations with a set of data that contains averages. Traders use this indicator in different ways. Some use it to plot resistance and support while others use it to generate buying and selling signals. Another use of Moving Averages is for determining optimal entry points in long-term investments. By studying the trends of Moving Averages, traders can identify favorable periods to initiate positions, aiming to capture potential future price appreciation. This approach allows investors to take advantage of the overall market direction and align their investments accordingly.

On very rare occasions a golden cross and a death cross can also occur. These are rare events that occur when a shorter-term moving average (such as the 50-day moving average) crosses above a longer-term moving average (such as the 200-day moving average) on a price chart. This event is considered bullish and is often interpreted as a positive signal for future price movements. It suggests that the asset's upward momentum may continue, potentially indicating a trend reversal or the start of an upward trend. Traders and investors often pay attention to golden crosses as they can influence buying and selling decisions. Death cross occurs when when a shorter-term moving average (such as the 50-day moving average) crosses below a longer-term moving average (such as the 200-day moving average) on a price chart. The death cross is considered a negative signal and is often interpreted as a potential indication of a downward trend or a trend reversal. Traders and investors may view the death cross as a sign to sell or take a more cautious approach to the asset.

How to apply moving average to your analysis?

1. Open a trading platform
2. Go to 'indicators'
3. Find the moving average indicator and apply it to your charts
4. Select your time period
5. Configure the moving average lines according to your trading strategy

How to use the Moving average indicator to make your decision?

a. Using moving average for buying signal-: when moving average is below the price line. It represents a possible bullish market.

b. Using moving average for selling signal-: when moving average is above the price line. It represents a possible bearish market.

c. Using moving average for holding signal-: when moving average moves through the price line. It signals price continuation and to hold the asset.

2. Bollinger bands

This indicator, though very complex in its name, is simply a tool to calculate price deviations. The bands comprise of three lines plotted in the charts, an upper, a middle and a lower one. The middle line is called the "middle band" and is typically a simple moving average (SMA) of the cryptocurrency's price over a certain period, such as 20 days. SMA is nothing but an average of the prices of a coin in that particular time plotted in a chart and indicated through a line. Upper and lower bands are plotted in relation to the middle band. Their position is calculated based on the standard deviation of the price from the middle band. The standard deviation is a statistical measure of volatility. By default, the upper band is set to two standard deviations above the middle band, while the lower band is set to two standard deviations below it.

When the price moves close to the upper band, it may indicate that the cryptocurrency is overbought, meaning it could be due for a downward correction. Conversely, when the price approaches the lower band, it may suggest that the cryptocurrency is oversold, indicating a potential upward rebound.

The width between the upper and lower bands fluctuates depending on the price volatility of the cryptocurrency. When the price is more volatile, the bands widen, and when the price is less volatile, the bands contract.

3. MACD

the MACD indicator is derived from the difference between two exponential moving averages (EMAs) of the cryptocurrency's price. EMAs mean the moving averages of shorter periods of time. The most commonly used EMAs are the 12-day EMA and the 26-day EMA. The MACD line is calculated by subtracting the 26-day EMA from the 12-day EMA.

Additionally, a signal line, which is typically a 9-day EMA of the MACD line, is plotted on the chart. The signal line helps smooth out the MACD line and generates trading signals.

The MACD indicator also includes a histogram, which represents the difference between the MACD line and the signal line. The histogram provides visual clues about the strength and direction of the price momentum. The MACD (Moving Average Convergence Divergence) is an indicator that in simple terms understands the relative movement between to moving averages. The convergence and divergence in MACD is studied to make sense of trends and generate buying and selling signals.

Traders use the MACD indicator in several ways. Here are a few common strategies:

When the MACD is in positive territory, it indicates that the short-term Moving Average is positioned above the long-term average, suggesting an upward trend in the market. Traders often view this as a bullish signal and may consider it a potential buy signal.

Conversely, when the MACD dips into negative territory, it signifies that the short-term Moving Average is below the long-term Moving Average. This suggests a downward trend in the market. When the MACD shifts from positive to negative, some traders interpret it as an indication to sell their positions, expecting further price declines.

How to use the Moving average indicator to make your decision?

a. Using MACD for buying signal-: when the fast line intersects the slow line from underneath, it gives a buying signal towards a possible bullish market.

b. Using moving average for selling signal-: when the fast line intersects the slow line from above, it gives a selling signal towards a possible bearish market.

c. Using moving average for holding signal-: when moving average moves through the price line. It signals price continuation and to hold the asset.

2. RSI- Relative Strength Index

The RSI measures the magnitude of recent price changes to determine whether a cryptocurrency is overbought or oversold. It is plotted on a scale ranging from 0 to 100.

The RSI is calculated based on the average gain and average loss over a specified period, typically 14 days. The formula involves comparing the average gain (the sum of positive price changes) and the average loss (the sum of negative price changes) over the specified period. The resulting value is then transformed into an oscillator that fluctuates between 0 and 100.

Traders use the RSI indicator in a few different ways:

1. **Overbought and Oversold Levels:** The RSI provides overbought and oversold levels at 70 and 30, respectively. When the RSI rises above 70, it suggests that the cryptocurrency may be overbought, meaning its price has risen too much and a potential correction or reversal could occur. Conversely, when the RSI drops below 30, it suggests that the cryptocurrency may be oversold, indicating a potential upward rebound.

2. **Divergence:** Traders also look for divergences between the RSI and the price. For example, if the price is making higher highs while the RSI is making lower highs, it may indicate a potential trend reversal or weakening momentum.

3. **Centerline Crossover:** The centerline of the RSI is typically set at 50. When the RSI crosses above 50, it suggests bullish momentum, indicating potential buying opportunities. Conversely, when the RSI crosses below 50, it suggests bearish momentum, indicating potential selling opportunities.

Example:

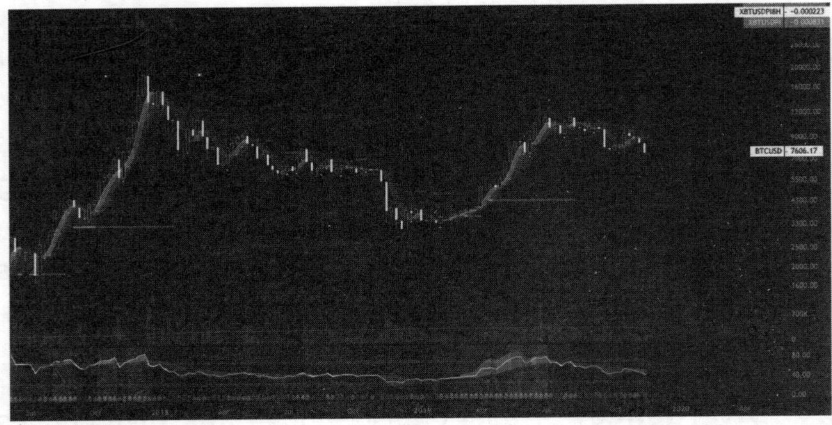

5. Volume based indicator

Volume represents the level of buyer-seller activity in a specific stock. Analyzing volume involves considering the interaction between price and volume. When the price exceeds its moving average, it indicates an increase in trade volume, while a drop below the moving average suggests a decrease in trade volume. Remember, volume reflects buyer-seller interest. Low trade volumes can lead to false breakouts, while high trade volumes are more likely to indicate genuine breakouts.

Let's consider different scenarios to understand the relationship between price, volume, and market trends:

1. The first scenario involves trading within a support-resistance range using technical analysis. If a breakout occurs, it's crucial to check the volume. A breakout accompanied by above-average or near-average volume is considered a valid breakout, whereas lower

volume suggests a fake breakout. This situation, with high volume and high price, creates a strong bullish trend.

2. The second scenario occurs when volume remains above or near the average line, but the price drops and reaches its support level. This situation indicates a strong bearish trend in the market.

3. The third scenario occurs when the price continues to rise towards its pivot or resistance line, but the volume declines. This signals an early indication of a trend reversal under a weak trend. The reduced interest of buyers and sellers, reflected in the lower volume, contributes to this weak trend.

4. The fourth scenario is characterized by both the price and volume decreasing. This indicates a reversal under a weak trend, where both the buyer-seller interest (volume) and the price decline.

In the first and second scenarios, where the volume is above the average line, it influences the formation of price trends. Understanding these trends requires strategies and analysis, which will be covered in the subsequent chapters.

Example:

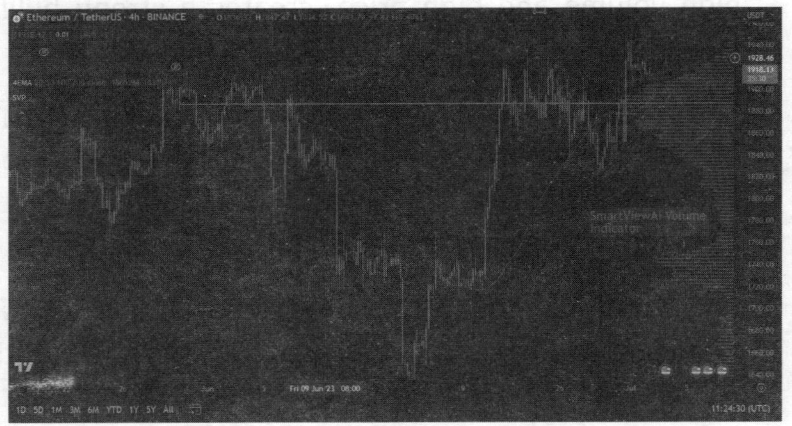
Ethereum / TetherUS · 4h · BINANCE
SmartViewAI Volume Indicator
Fri 09 Jun '23 08:00
1D 5D 1M 3M 6M YTD 1Y 5Y All
11:24:30 (UTC)

Chapter 5

How to choose the right cryptocurrency?

The present times has seen a burgeoning trend in the crypto sector to the point that every few minutes a new cryptocurrency is taking birth. At present there are around 20,000 cryptocurrencies in circulation. In such a scenario it is extremely difficult to keep track of all coins and find out the right cryptocurrency for oneself. On the contrary the coins that are well known, have already been mined enough to their capacity and some of the biggest opportunities in the gains have been lost around them. So the question is how in the midst of all the confusion, one chooses the projects that have a long run into the future, are not part of fraudulent activities, are profitable and have real use cases.

I believe that just like making any other choice in our lives, the choice for cryptocurrency should also come with the right balance of our heart and mind. When you begin to select the right cryptocurrency as a project for your investment or trading, you should first start with your heart. Research on the major sectors in which cryptocurrency are categorized into. For example, the major categories include, education, health, Tourism, real estate etc. Once you select the category of your choice, you should begin to explore the set of coins that are available under it. Let's say for a certain category Health, there are around 23 coins on a trading platform. Now once you have the list of coins, you shall start performing fundamental as well as technical analysis on the crypto assets. To begin with, assess the time goals of your investment, whether you will be trading short term or holding the asset for long term. If you wish to hold the asset long term, you should focus more on the fundamental analysis and if you wish to trade intraday or short term, focus on technical analysis more. However, all in all, basic fundamental and technical analysis should be conducted for every investment or trade that you make.

Consult Professionals: If you are uncertain about investing in cryptocurrencies, it may be helpful to seek advice from financial professionals or cryptocurrency experts who can provide guidance based on your specific financial situation and investment goals.

Understanding the landscape of cryptocurrencies requires a comprehensive framework to evaluate various aspects of the projects. This framework will help provide an overview and guide your decision-making process.

1. **Who is who?** This stage involves researching the project owners, creation dates, and expiry dates to gather information about the project. Consider the age of the cryptocurrency and its track record. Assessing the risk appetite is crucial here, as the longer a

cryptocurrency has been live, the more established it becomes. Reviewing whitepapers can provide valuable insights into the project's purpose, vision, and underlying technology. However, it is important to rewrite the content in a way that avoids plagiarism and AI detection.

2. **Find the whitepaper:** A whitepaper serves as a document that outlines a cryptocurrency project's purpose, vision, and philosophy. It presents detailed statistics, graphs, and algorithms that describe the project's resources and technology through technical analyses. A well-written whitepaper will address the project's fundamentals, its unique solution to existing problems, and the utility it offers. It should also provide information about the cryptocurrency's supply, functionality, and a timeline for future development.

3. **Website:** Evaluating a project's website is essential to assess its functionality and user interface. Look for a website that offers a smooth user experience and lacks technical glitches, as this indicates the project's competence and professionalism.

4. **Project activity:** Examining the project's activity helps determine its reliability and legitimacy. Look for indicators such as social media activity, community engagement, developer activity, and trading volume. Active social media handles, regularly updated websites, and routine content publication can be positive signs. Additionally, vibrant communities on platforms like Reddit, Discord, and Telegram indicate a well-functioning project. Developer activity on platforms like GitHub is also important, as it

demonstrates ongoing progress and collaboration. Adequate trading volume reflects interest and helps maintain the cryptocurrency's stability and liquidity.

5. **Transparency:** Legitimate projects prioritize transparency and accountability. Developers should share sufficient information with investors, have a platform for addressing concerns and questions promptly, and provide detailed analyses and statistics about the cryptocurrency and its blockchain. Transparency allows investors to gauge the experience, expertise, and track record of the project's creators.

6. **Team:** Assess the developers' expertise, vision, and prior work profiles. A capable and experienced team increases the credibility of the project.

7. **Community:** Pay attention to the public interest in the project, as a higher level of community engagement indicates potential value. However, ensure that the hype surrounding a project aligns with its real worth, which you have determined through the previous stages.

Fundamental analysis incorporates metrics such as financial, on-chain, and project metrics to assess the viability and potential of a cryptocurrency. Technical analysis involves indicators such as moving averages, MACD, RSI, volume-based indicators, and Bollinger bands to analyze price trends and patterns.

When buying cryptocurrency, it is advisable to spread your purchases across different price points, such as the current price, 10% lower, and 20% lower. This diversification helps manage assets effectively.

Determining the right time to invest in cryptocurrencies requires careful consideration of individual circumstances, risk tolerance, and thorough research. Cryptocurrency markets are highly volatile and influenced by various factors. A long-term investment approach is often more suitable, allowing you to ride out market fluctuations and potentially benefit from growth over time. Stay informed about the technology, fundamentals, market trends, regulatory developments, and risks associated with the chosen cryptocurrencies.

Implementing a dollar-cost averaging strategy, rather than investing a lump sum at once, can help mitigate the impact of short-term market volatility. Additionally, managing risk by diversifying your investment portfolio across different asset classes, including cryptocurrencies, is crucial.

Focus on understanding the fundamentals and long-term potential of the cryptocurrencies you consider investing in. Look for projects with solid technology, a strong development team, real-world use cases, and widespread adoption potential. Timing the market perfectly is challenging, so concentrate on the project's merits rather than attempting to predict short-term market movements.

Thorough research and continuous education are vital before venturing into cryptocurrency investments. It is crucial to gain a comprehensive understanding of the specific cryptocurrencies you are interested in, as well as the broader market dynamics. Stay informed about the underlying technology, project fundamentals, market trends, regulatory developments, and potential risks associated with the chosen cryptocurrencies. By acquiring this knowledge, you can make more informed investment decisions.

Implementing a dollar-cost averaging (DCA) strategy can be beneficial when investing in cryptocurrencies. Instead of investing a lump sum at a specific time, DCA involves consistently investing a fixed amount at regular intervals, regardless of the cryptocurrency's price. This approach helps mitigate the impact of short-term market volatility by spreading out your investments over time. By sticking to a DCA strategy, you can potentially achieve a more balanced entry point and reduce the risk of making large investments during market peaks.

Managing risk is a critical aspect of any investment strategy, including cryptocurrency investments. Consider your risk tolerance and investment goals when deciding on your crypto investment strategy. Cryptocurrencies are known for their high volatility, which can lead to significant gains or substantial losses. Diversifying your investment portfolio across different asset classes, including cryptocurrencies, can help spread risk and minimize potential losses. By diversifying, you are less exposed to the fluctuations of any single asset or market.

When it comes to market timing, attempting to perfectly predict short-term market movements is challenging, even for experienced investors. Instead of focusing on short-term market timing, direct your attention to understanding the fundamental aspects and long-term potential of the cryptocurrencies you are considering. Look for projects with robust technology, a strong development team, real-world use cases, and the potential for widespread adoption. By assessing these factors, you can identify cryptocurrencies with solid foundations and long-term growth potential, which may offer more sustainable investment opportunities.

Remember, investing in cryptocurrencies involves inherent risks, and individual circumstances and risk tolerance should be carefully considered. It is advisable to consult with financial professionals and conduct thorough research before making any investment decisions.

Chapter 6:

Market timings

Before you even begin to trade, one question might be troubling you for sure. Your core of concern might be, but when do I buy and when do I sell? Who will tell me what is the right timing for both and if not ask from others, how will I know what to do and when to do it. I can understand how confusing it might all be. But trading is like piecing together a puzzle. All the pieces are in front of you, you only need to put them together and make sense out of it. The tool or concept that you use to answer these questions is market timing. Market timing refers to the strategy of attempting to predict the best moments to enter or exit a market, such as buying or selling cryptocurrencies, based on short-term price movements. Your entry and exit are the lifelines of your trading success. With a right entry you book the potential of a profit whereas with right exit you not only book profit but also target to mitigate loss. However, accurately timing the market consistently is extremely challenging, even for experienced investors, due to the inherent volatility and unpredictability of cryptocurrency markets. It's important to approach market timing with caution and consider the following points:

Understanding Volatility: Cryptocurrency markets are known for their high levels of volatility. Prices can experience rapid fluctuations within short periods, making it difficult to accurately predict short-term price movements. Timing the market based on short-term price changes can be risky and may lead to missed opportunities or potential losses.

Patience with Long-Term Focus: Instead of focusing on short-term market timing, consider taking a long-term investment approach when it comes to cryptocurrencies. Long-term investing allows you to ride out the volatility and potentially benefit from the growth of the overall market over time.

Fundamental Analysis: When considering an investment in cryptocurrencies, it's crucial to conduct fundamental analysis. Evaluate the underlying technology, the project's team and development roadmap, market adoption, and potential real-world use cases. By focusing on the long-term potential of a cryptocurrency based on its fundamentals, you can make more informed investment decisions rather than relying solely on short-term market timing.

Laddering: Laddering is a strategy that can help reduce risk and improve entry decisions in the volatile cryptocurrency market. Rather than attempting to time the perfect entry or exit point in one go, laddering involves gradually entering or exiting a position through a series of small trades. This approach helps mitigate the impact of market volatility and increases the likelihood of achieving a safer average entry or exit price.

For instance, let's consider the scenario where the price of Bitcoin is decreasing, but you anticipate a potential upward movement in the near future. Instead of trying to catch the absolute bottom, laddering allows you to enter your position gradually over a period of a few hours. By executing a series of small trades, you can establish an average entry price that is more secure compared to a single large entry.

Similarly, laddering can be employed to secure profits by exiting a position over time, without the need to pinpoint the exact market peak. Traders often set multiple price targets at which they will close a percentage of their position, ensuring they can capture profits along the way.

By implementing the laddering strategy, you can navigate the challenging task of timing the market perfectly. This approach provides a more measured and controlled approach to entering or exiting trades, reducing the risk associated with sudden market movements and increasing the potential for improved results.

Technical Analysis: Technical analysis (TA) plays a crucial role in trading and offers a diverse range of tools and techniques to generate trading signals. By mastering TA, traders can make informed decisions on when to enter or exit positions based on market trends and patterns.

One common strategy in TA involves identifying support and resistance levels. These levels are not fixed and can change over time. By drawing unbiased trendlines, traders can pinpoint key levels and intersections that can serve as potential entry or exit points for trades.

Chart patterns are another valuable aspect of TA. Recognizing patterns forming on price charts can provide insights into future price movements. If a pattern emerges, traders can observe its development and, if it confirms, be prepared to execute trades in the anticipated direction. Chart patterns often influence the movement of assets.

However, it's important to understand that even with technical analysis, achieving the perfect entry or exit point is unlikely. The key is to remain diligent and adhere to your trading strategy. It is possible to buy an asset that is trending upward, sell it at a profit, and then witness further upward movement after your exit. Although you may have missed additional gains, it is essential to remember that missing out on an opportunity is different from incurring a loss.

Indicators are valuable tools for identifying entry and exit points. They provide various insights depending on the specific indicators used. Traders often leverage indicators such as the Fibonacci indicator, pivot points, and other mathematical-based indicators to help guide their decision-making process.

To optimize your trading strategy, it is essential to experiment with different indicators and identify which ones work best for you. By combining technical analysis tools, chart patterns, and indicators, traders can enhance their ability to identify favorable entry and exit points in the market. However, it is crucial to continue learning, adapt to changing market conditions, and exercise prudent risk management to achieve long-term trading success.

Dollar-Cost Averaging (DCA): DCA is a strategy where you invest a fixed amount at regular intervals, regardless of the cryptocurrency's price. This approach can help mitigate the impact of short-term price fluctuations and potentially provide a more balanced entry point over time. DCA is often considered a more prudent approach for long-term cryptocurrency investments.

Risk Management: Assess your risk tolerance and investment goals before investing in cryptocurrencies. Only invest an amount you are willing to lose, as the market is highly volatile. Diversify your investment portfolio across different asset classes to manage risk effectively.

Seek Professional Advice: If you are uncertain about market timing or investing in cryptocurrencies, consider consulting with financial professionals or cryptocurrency experts. They can provide insights based on their expertise and help guide you through the investment process.

1. Research and Analysis: Stay updated with the latest news, developments, and trends in the cryptocurrency industry. Conduct thorough research on the specific cryptocurrencies you are interested in, including their technology, team, partnerships, adoption, and market sentiment. Technical analysis and chart patterns may also provide insights into potential price movements.

2. Use Technical Indicators: Utilize technical indicators and chart analysis tools to identify potential entry or exit points. Common indicators include moving averages, relative strength index (RSI), MACD, and Bollinger Bands. However, it's important to note that technical analysis is not foolproof and should be used in conjunction with other analysis methods.

3. Develop a Trading Strategy: Establish a clear trading strategy based on your risk tolerance, investment goals, and time horizon. Determine your entry and exit points, profit targets, and stop-loss levels. Stick to your strategy and avoid making impulsive decisions based on short-term market fluctuations.

4. Monitor Market Sentiment: Pay attention to market sentiment, as it can influence short-term price movements. Monitor social media platforms, online communities, and cryptocurrency news outlets to gauge investor sentiment and market expectations. However, be cautious as sentiment can be biased and subject to manipulation.

5. Use Limit Orders: When executing trades, consider using limit orders instead of market orders. Limit orders allow you to set a specific price at which you want to buy or sell a cryptocurrency. This approach can help you avoid overpaying or underselling during volatile market conditions.

6. Keep Emotions in Check: Emotional decision-making can lead to poor market timing. Avoid making impulsive decisions driven by fear or greed. Stick to your predetermined strategy and remain disciplined, even during periods of market volatility.

7. Learn from Mistakes: Continuously evaluate your trading decisions and learn from both successful and unsuccessful trades. Keep a trading journal to track your trades, record the reasoning behind your decisions, and identify areas for improvement. Continuously educate yourself about cryptocurrencies and the market. Stay open to learning from your

experiences and adapt your strategies as needed.

8. Dollar-Cost Averaging (DCA): Implement a DCA strategy by investing a fixed amount at regular intervals, regardless of the cryptocurrency's price. This approach allows you to mitigate the impact of short-term price fluctuations and potentially achieve a more balanced entry point over time.

Remember, every investment strategy carries risks, and a particular strategy is not a guaranteed method for success. It's crucial to conduct thorough research, monitor market trends, and consider your risk tolerance before implementing any trading strategy in the cryptocurrency market.

CHAPTER 7

MISSION MILLION WITH CRYPTO

As discussed earlier there are multiple ways of earning money with cryptocurrency including but not limited to trading, investment, staking, interest and mining. One can try a combination of these avenues or focus on a particular one to build wealth for themselves. Hereon, I will try to explain each strategy in depth.

1. Cryptocurrency SIP

You may be someone who doesn't understand the term SIP or maybe someone who knows SIP but has never done it before. You might also be someone looking to better your SIP strategy with this information. No matter where you stand right now. Through this, I will take you to the practical understanding and application of SIP. And I will also try to answer the questions that are most frequently asked by investors. There is also a certain pride I feel in being one of the pioneers in introducing this strategy in India.

SIP is a systematic Investment Plan. The process through which one to invest money regularly in a fund, a group of funds or any other securities. One of the biggest benefits of SIP is that it enables one to invest for a goal through systematic plan, even with a smaller chunk of money. Given that it is planned and executed through consistency, SIP employs one of the most productive tools of finance, compounding. A normal notion is that to make big money you need big money. SIPs are these notion breakers as it allows the investor to make big money, through even as small an investment of INR 500. SIPs are customizable, so you can decide on the investment amount, time and avenue according to your style, comfort and pace. You can invest in SIPs on centralized or decentralized platforms. SIPs are long term investments and the funds for the same shall be the ones that you are comfortable in keeping aside for a longer period of time. Since SIPs are based on the principle of compounding time is a very important factor that should be considered in the process. Don't expect your money to grow in 10-15 days, each SIP goal differs from person to person and with the goal differs its type, principal amount, interest rate and time period.

One thing that I always say is invest into trends and invest before anyone else. I want to make this strategy accessible and executable to everyone, so I'll start with a sum that is significant yet not too heavy on the pocket. The monthly investment that you need in order to become a millionaire is $20 dollars. If you invest this money every month into an SIP of a cryptocurrency at an ROI of 60% you will be shocked to see how much money will it account to in the future. In a time period of 20 years, your entire sum will reach $51,130,220.97, in short account to 51 million dollars. Now you might think that this is some sort of a scam, it is impossible to make such money with just 20 dollars. This is where compound interest comes to play. But let's say you would like to commit a lesser amount to your monthly SIP, let's say $10, even then in a course of 20 years you can make . One of the best ages to start investment is the age of 25. This is when most of the people start earning and are looking for avenues to grow their money. So, I would also say that SIP is one of the best avenues for such aspiring investors.

Till now we have explored the power of compounding in terms of SIP but now let's discover the power of staking for the same. Let's assume that there are two people Ram and Shyam. Ram and Shyam both invests $1000 dollars and buy 50 tokens each of TOMO. Ram awaits a price appreciation of the token and holds it in anticipation of the same for a year. On the contrary Shyam stakes his 50 TOMO tokens and holds them for a year. Staking is when you lock crypto assets for a set period of time to help support the operation of a blockchain. In return for staking your crypto, you earn more cryptocurrency. Many blockchain assets use proof of staking. Under this system, network participants who want to support the blockchain by validating new transactions and adding new blocks must "stake" set sums of cryptocurrency.

Staking helps ensure that only legitimate data and transactions are added to a blockchain. Participants trying to earn a chance to validate new transactions offer to lock up sums of cryptocurrency in staking as a form of insurance.

After a year, let's assume TOMO token appreciated to $60, making a profit for both Ram and Shyam. However Ram's profit for that year was $3000 while that of Shyam was

$6000. The question now arises, if both of them had similar no. of tokens, similar principal sum and similar time period of holding, why were the outputs different. The answer to this is staking. While the no. of tokens with Ram stayed the same at 50, Shyam's tokens increased to 100 with staking. Shyam's staking came with an APY of 100%. His no. of tokens grew to 100 and his output became 100x$60=$6000. After 2 years if the same cases are compared, Ram's output will be $6,000 but Shyam's output will be $24,000 as his profit is growing based on both price and staking. The same applies to a price depreciation as well. Taking the same principal amounts of $1000 each and 50 token each. Ram will drop to $500 based on the price downward movement but Shyam will be cushioned against the fall through the power of staking. Since his no. of tokens with staking and its 100% APY grew from 50 to 100, each token now priced at 10 dollars, his output will maintain at $1000. Whereas Ram's no. of tokens remains 50 and therefore his output equals $500. In the third case, if prices remain same, even in that case, Shyam will benefit with staking as the no. of tokens will still double to increase his profit. Whereas Ram's will maintain the same principal amount.

Benefits of Investing in a SIP

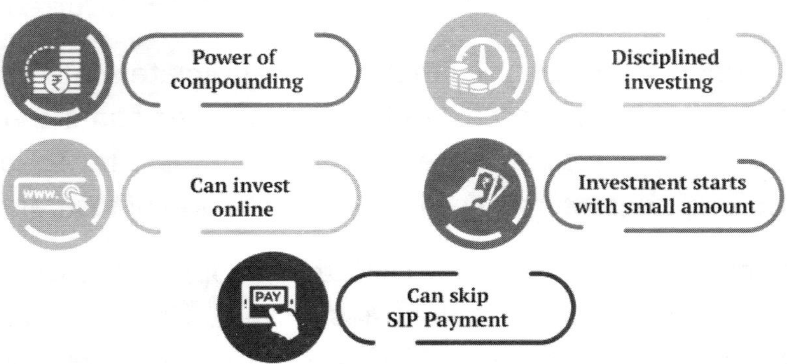

Where should you invest in SIP?

I always advise people to never invest hefty amounts in centralized platforms. I do not promote these third part SIP platforms as there is no guarantee that they will exist in the near future. But I also understand that at the beginning it takes time to learn about the technology, different platforms, storage etc. So I can say this with small amounts that are not your lifetime savings but something you can use to get started, you can start with a centralized platform.

Choose a platform that you can establish through research to be of trust. Once you learn the process and you start growing, you can shift your sum to a decentralized exchange (DEX) platform. Normally DEX also offers higher APYs.

SIP has been confused by a lot of exchanges. To simplify I just say, you buy a coin, discover a good APY and then deploy it for staking. This is SIP for me, a good systematically planned investment.

1. Dollar cost averaging

Cryptocurrencies are known for their volatility and swift movements in the market. When you invest with a lump sum amount in the cryptocurrency or any security for that sake, your big profits only follow with big investments calculated at right timings. These timings require a lot of calculations, capital which in return require experience and expertise.

However for most of the investors such large Lump sum investments can be little difficult to arrange and for beginners it can be like playing darts in a dark room. With no prior knowledge of where to strike and when to strike.

This is where Dollar cost averaging helps to ease out the price discrepancies of the crypto market.

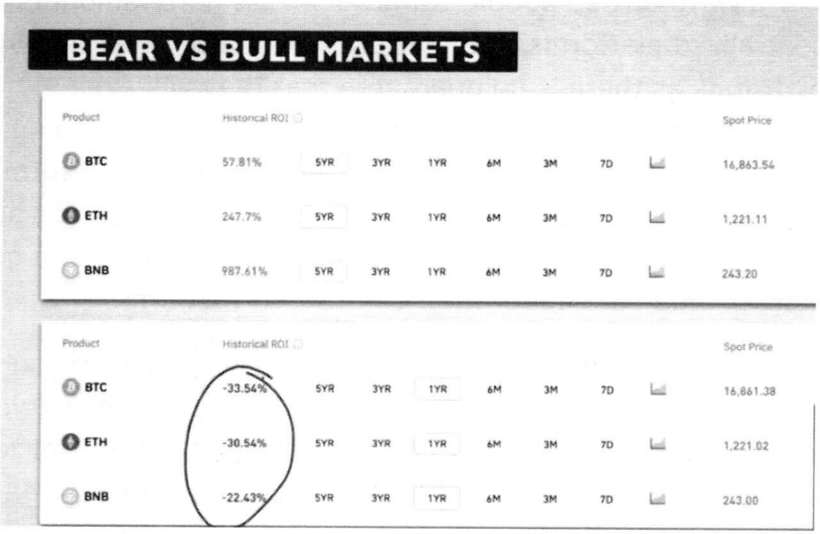

BEAR VS BULL MARKETS

Product	Historical ROI								Spot Price
BTC	57.81%	5YR	3YR	1YR	6M	3M	7D		16,863.54
ETH	247.7%	5YR	3YR	1YR	6M	3M	7D		1,221.11
BNB	987.61%	5YR	3YR	1YR	6M	3M	7D		243.20

Product	Historical ROI								Spot Price
BTC	-33.54%	5YR	3YR	1YR	6M	3M	7D		16,861.38
ETH	-30.54%	5YR	3YR	1YR	6M	3M	7D		1,221.02
BNB	-22.43%	5YR	3YR	1YR	6M	3M	7D		243.00

- Dollar-cost averaging is the practice of systematically investing equal amounts of money at regular intervals, regardless of the price of a security.

Let me explain it using this example. Let's say you systematically plan to buy gold every month irrespective of its price fluctuations. Now, gold moves in both directions, upwards and downwards. When you invest systematically for a long period of time, your output becomes the average of of all highs and lows balancing each other. The question that arises is how does one decide when to invest. For this, one needs to set a particular date and time interval based upon some research and analysis. The primary goal in dollar cost averaging always remains to build savings and wealth over the long term while ignoring short-term volatility.

On the contrary when a lump sum investment is made, the only way to earn a good return is if the investor buys big, buys early and buys at the least.

Why Do Some Investors Use Dollar-Cost Averaging?

The primary benefit of utilizing dollar-cost averaging is its ability to mitigate the detrimental impact of investor psychology and market timing on an investment portfolio. By adhering to a dollar-cost averaging strategy, investors can prevent the potential negative consequences of making impulsive decisions driven by greed or fear, such as purchasing more assets when prices are surging or hastily selling off assets during market declines. Instead, dollar-cost averaging compels investors to concentrate on consistently contributing a predetermined amount of money at regular intervals, disregarding the fluctuations in the price of the target security.

Benefits of Dollar-Cost Averaging

- Dollar cost averaging can lower the average amount you spend on investments.
- It reinforces the practice of investing regularly to build wealth over time.
- It's automatic and can take concerns about when to invest out of your hands.
- It removes the pitfalls of market timing, such as buying only when prices have already risen.
- It can ensure that you're already in the market and ready to buy when events send prices higher.
- It takes emotion out of your investing and prevents you from potentially damaging your portfolio's returns.

Example of Dollar- Cost Averaging

There was no way for Joe to know the best time to buy. By using dollar-cost averaging, though, he was able to take advantage of several price drops despite the fact that the share price increased to over $11. He ended up with more shares (47.71) at a lower average price ($10.48).

Let's say you decide to invest ₹50,000 in a particular stock over the course of 10 months using a dollar-cost averaging strategy. You plan to invest ₹5,000 at the beginning of each month, regardless of the stock's price. Here are the monthly prices of the stock and the number of shares you acquire each month:

Month 1: Price per share = ₹100, Shares acquired = ₹5,000 / ₹100 = 50 shares

Month 2: Price per share = ₹80, Shares acquired = ₹5,000 / ₹80 = 62.5 shares (rounded down to 62 shares)

Month 3: Price per share = ₹120, Shares acquired = ₹5,000 / ₹120 = 41.67 shares (rounded down to 41 shares)

Month 4: Price per share = ₹150, Shares acquired = ₹5,000 / ₹150 = 33.33 shares (rounded down to 33 shares)

Month 5: Price per share = ₹180, Shares acquired = ₹5,000 / ₹180 = 27.78 shares (rounded down to 27 shares)

Month 6: Price per share = ₹200, Shares acquired = ₹5,000 / ₹200 = 25 shares

Month 7: Price per share = ₹250, Shares acquired = ₹5,000 / ₹250 = 20 shares

Month 8: Price per share = ₹300, Shares acquired =

₹5,000 / ₹300 = 16.67 shares (rounded down to 16 shares)

Month 9: Price per share = ₹280, Shares acquired = ₹5,000 / ₹280 = 17.86 shares (rounded down to 17 shares)

Month 10: Price per share = ₹260, Shares acquired = ₹5,000 / ₹260 = 19.23 shares (rounded down to 19 shares)

After 10 months, you have accumulated a total of 353.35 shares by investing a total of ₹50,000. Now, let's assume the stock's price increases to ₹350 per share. By multiplying the number of shares acquired in each month with the current share price, we can calculate the current value of your investment:

Month 1: 50 shares * ₹350 = ₹17,500

Month 2: 62 shares * ₹350 = ₹21,700

Month 3: 41 shares * ₹350 = ₹14,350

Month 4: 33 shares * ₹350 = ₹11,550

Month 5: 27 shares * ₹350 = ₹9,450

Month 6: 25 shares * ₹350 = ₹8,750

Month 7: 20 shares * ₹350 = ₹7,000

Month 8: 16 shares * ₹350 = ₹5,600

Month 9: 17 shares * ₹350 = ₹5,950

Month 10: 19 shares * ₹350 = ₹6,650

The current value of your investment would be ₹108,500, which represents a 117% increase from your initial investment of ₹50,000. This demonstrates the power of dollar-cost averaging, as you were able to take advantage of both lower and higher prices throughout the 10-month period, resulting in a favorable return on investment.

1. Crypto mining-

Mining is often understood in terms of extracting ores and minerals from earth. Mining here, however, represents a different connotation, one that means creating more cryptocurrency while solving complex mathematical problems. There was a time when you could mine cryptocurrency with simple hardware at your home but with more people buying and mining these coins, the complexity of both have significantly increased over time.

Who are the miners?

Miners are entities that solve computational problems and validate transactions in the block chain network. In the early days of cryptocurrency, even CPUs could be used to mine coins.

Are miners people or computers?

Miners are typically individuals or organizations who own or operate hardwares and computer systems that can perform the mining task. While miners operate the hardware, the actual process of mining is performed by the computer or the machine in the system. The process of mining requires the machines to solve mathematical problems which are increasing in complexity with time. For instance cryptocurrencies like Bitcoin, miners use their computer systems, which can include CPUs (Central Processing Units), GPUs (Graphics Processing Units), or ASICs (Application-Specific Integrated Circuits). Miners invest in the necessary hardware, software, and infrastructure to support the mining process. They configure and maintain their mining equipment, ensure proper cooling and power supply, and monitor the mining operations for optimal performance.

Is Crypto mining worth it?

Evaluating the profitability of crypto mining involves various factors. Whether one opts for CPU, GPU, ASIC miners, or cloud mining, key considerations include the hash rate of the mining rig, power consumption, and associated costs. It is worth noting that crypto mining machines typically consume significant electricity and generate considerable heat.

To illustrate, an average ASIC miner, for instance, may consume approximately 72 terawatts of power to mine a single bitcoin within a ten-minute timeframe. These metrics are subject to change as mining technology advances and the difficulty level increases.

In addition to the initial cost of the mining equipment,

it is crucial to factor in ongoing expenses such as electricity consumption, local electricity rates, and cooling requirements, particularly for GPU and ASIC mining rigs.

Furthermore, assessing the difficulty level of the targeted cryptocurrency is essential to determine the potential profitability of the mining operation.

Here are some key considerations for earning from mining:

1. Selecting the Right Cryptocurrency: Choosing the right cryptocurrency to mine is the most important step. There are some coins that are highly competitive like Bitcoin and Ethereum and these coins now require sophisticated hardware which may not be possible for a beginner. So based on your level of entry, capital and expertise, you can choose the right cryptocurrency for you.

2. Mining Equipment: Invest in specialized mining hardware, such as ASICs or GPUs, depending on the cryptocurrency you choose to mine. ASICs are designed specifically for mining certain cryptocurrencies, while GPUs offer more flexibility but may have lower efficiency. Consider factors like hash rate, power consumption, and cost when selecting mining equipment.

3. Mining Pool: Mining pool is when miners pool their equipment's and perform mining with the help of each other. With rising complexity the hardware requirement has also changed. Combining system of each individual to build a stronger one in unity can increase the chances of a successful mining. When the mining completes, the rewards are distributed equally

amongst the members.

4. Mining Software and Configuration: Set up mining software to connect your mining hardware to the network. Configure the software with the appropriate mining parameters and optimize it for performance. Stay updated with the latest mining software and firmware updates to ensure efficiency.

4. Initial coin offering

There have been some popular ways of raising funding in the market, these include IPOs, crowdfunding, government funding etc. The main problem with these fund raising avenues was that a small startup, or an idea could not receive them as it needed validation and approval through a whole cumbersome process. Funding requires you to reach a certain level and certain numbers. A new member that surpassed all these limitations, recently entered the picture and this is called ICOs or Initial Coin Offerings. They have emerged as a groundbreaking crowdfunding method utilized by cryptocurrency and blockchain projects to secure capital directly from the public. This innovative approach allows startups to circumvent the traditional fundraising process and directly access funding from a global pool of investors.

During an ICO, a project or company issues and sells new digital tokens or cryptocurrencies to investors in exchange for established cryptocurrencies like Bitcoin or Ethereum, and sometimes even traditional fiat currencies. These tokens, built on blockchain platforms such as Ethereum, serve as digital assets or utilities within the project's ecosystem.

How are ICOs better than traditional fundraising options?

ICOs have especially opened up a lot of space for startup growth as now these small companies can raise funds directly from the public. The qualifications required to enlist an IPO were suitable only for the companies that were well established leaving startups and smaller companies out of the picture. With the coming of ICOs, startups now have an alternative avenue to raise funds, bypassing the need for traditional intermediaries like venture capitalists or banks. This democratized approach enables early-stage companies to tap into funding sources that may have been previously out of reach. The inherent nature of ICOs allows startups to attract investors from around the globe. By leveraging the widespread interest in the cryptocurrency and blockchain space, startups can connect with a diverse and expansive network of potential backers, expanding their funding prospects significantly. Launching an ICO often garners substantial media attention and publicity for startups. This heightened visibility helps raise awareness about the project, its unique value proposition, and its potential impact. Consequently, it can attract additional investors and users who are captivated by the project's vision. ICOs foster the creation of dedicated communities comprised of token holders who possess a vested interest in the project's success. These communities can offer invaluable feedback, unwavering support, and actively contribute to the project's ongoing development and growth. Meaningful engagement with this community can result in fruitful partnerships, collaborations, and a continuous feedback loop that fuels progress. By issuing tokens through an ICO, startups can establish a distinctive digital asset that holds intrinsic value within their ecosystem. These tokens can be designed to provide access to exclusive products or services, offer incentives for user participation, or confer ownership rights within the project. The utilization of tokens not only drives demand but also imbues the startup's offerings with inherent value and utility. ICO participants often enjoy early access to a project's products, services, or features. This advantageous position cultivates a loyal user base and facilitates iterative improvements based on user feedback and preferences, enabling startups to fine-tune their offerings and enhance user experience. ICOs have emerged as a pioneering force in funding cutting-edge projects within the cryptocurrency and blockchain realm. By participating in ICOs, startups actively contribute to the progress and advancement of transformative technologies, decentralized applications, and novel business models, thereby fostering innovation on a global scale.

Chapter 8

seven lessons

Cryptocurrency is a recent advancement in our world. There are confusions, explanations and a world of their continuous dialogues. I have tried my best to clear the confusions related to the knowhows of cryptocurrency. How to invest, where to invest, when to invest and even the best possible strategic way to building wealth with this wonderful asset. But however exciting and wonderful the world of cryptocurrency is, it also is daunting to do all this alone. Building money and assets require consistent efforts, knowledge; and through trial and errors, mistakes and lessons. You can't get it right every time. But you can get better with time. So you must learn and grow with each experience. However if there is someone who has been in the field for a longer time than you, who has tested the waters before you and whom you can trust to guide your path, it is always wise to take help and advice from them. Since you are my dear reader, I take upon the responsibility to provide value to you through my journey. It's been quite some time since I have been a part of the financial markets. In my initial years I had no one to explain things to me. I had a client who helped me with the very initial setup but I had to understand everything on my own after that. Over the years I have experienced a lot, experimented a lot and learnt a lot. My journey has taught me many things and it is these lessons that I am about to share with you. Even if it is through this book, I would like to pass on what I have gathered through this time and help you with it.

I am going to share my real life lessons with you. I have tried my best to sum up the entire context of my learnings into seven consolidated lessons. Adding on, these are not just the learnings I have made through these years, these are the lessons that I have compared with those of world's renowned leaders. They will help you to prune losses, improve profits and become a smart and a better investor.

1. **Always use stop loss-** I have seen most of the people with a lopsided perception of trading in their minds. There were times when cryptocurrency, Bitcoin, Ethereum were not so popular in the market and just after these assets made their way into the television conversations, being mentioned by renowned names like Elon musk and Jeff Bezos, this is when things changed for cryptocurrency. It became part of the common parlance and the masses rushed towards investing in the hot trade. However this half picture and hasty trades revealed something deeper. We always expect a profit and deny the possibility of a loss. And it is this denial that can lead to major losses when you trade. For some people, who try their hands for the first time in the market, call it beginner's luck as they

just see the bullish trend of the market and they may just cash in on its profits. But for such luck doesn't always last in the volatility of the crypto market, we should prepare for both sides of the trade.

As I said, when we trade, our excitement of making a profit overshadows the possibility of a loss. Let's assume that you buy bitcoin at 50,000 INR (not pertaining to current rates) and you anticipate to make a profit when its price hits 60,000 INR. And let's assume you do make a profit with the trade. On the flip side, let's say the bitcoin drops to 40,000 INR and before you could check or sell, the price had already slipped well below the point that you had considered the safe zone. This is where stop loss comes into the picture. Stop loss is a tool, a barrier that is used to protect you against trade losses. Sometimes when the price starts to dip we wait for a reversal and in this anticipation the trade bears losses. Tools are discovered and created to avoid the high interference of human emotions during such times. When you use stop loss you prepare to cushion yourself against the worst while waiting for the best to happen. In a trade of bitcoin which was bought at 50,000 INR, let's assume you decide to apply a stop loss at 48000 INR. As soon as the loss hits 48,000 the tool will automatically get you out of the trade and protect you against any further losses. There are certain cases where the need for a fixed stop loss becomes void as the prices begin to roar on the profit side. In this case you should use a trailing stop loss. A trailing stop loss is a way to protect your profits when trading. It automatically adjusts the stop loss level as the price of a security goes up in your favor. It's different from a regular stop loss because it moves with the market instead of staying at a fixed price. The trailing stop loss stays a certain distance or percentage below the highest price the security has reached since you started the trade or last adjusted the stop loss level.

A stop loss and trailing stop loss protects you on both ends of the trade. Thus it is always advisable to look at the full picture, analyze profits and losses, deploy tools for reassurance and then trade.

2. **Don't jump into the fire-** Trades are an easy prey to human emotions. Fear and greed are two dominant emotions that a trader feels most strongly. When the price goes up, one fears missing out, greeds to book the profits. Similarly when the prices go down, the trader fears a loss and hastes to sell his assets. These trades being emotionally charged, are dangerous and can lead to significant losses. If you see an asset pumping in the market and you might feel the need to buy it at the current price. Even if you wait it out, the anticipation of profit takes control over your rational mind, pushing you to buy more coins at higher and higher prices. But what about the dip that follows this high. This is how you could burn your money by jumping into the fire. I have also seen people entering the market without knowing where to enter, when to enter and even why to enter. They just hear about a market dump or pump and they enter without any prior know hows. Even if these hasty traders make money a time or two, they will most likely experience crashes that can burn their entire portfolios into nothing with just one move. The best way to go about in this situation is to study the given asset under fundamental and technical analysis first, study its charts, numbers and price action. These tools gives us objectivity and a real

picture around the asset. Thus while trading one must always look at things objectively rather than riding on the emotions and jumping in to the fire.

3. **Don't store money on exchanges-** Exchange platforms work to facilitate exchange of money with cryptocurrency and vice versa. These exchange platforms are not meant to store your funds. However most of the people keep their funds in store for long periods of time thinking that the platforms are safe havens for their money. This assumption is a far cry from truth. Consider this, you are only entitled as an owner of a piece of land where you hold it in papers and in a way a person who holds the papers to the land is its rightful owner. Similarly, these platforms and the funds on them are on paper under the owner's holdings. In future if the platform shuts down, your funds can go down with them (unless stated otherwise by the platform owners). By storing funds on an exchange, you become a creditor of that exchange. If the exchange becomes insolvent or faces financial difficulties, there is a risk that your funds may be subject to insolvency proceedings or become inaccessible.

Cryptocurrency exchanges are also prime targets for hackers due to the significant amounts of digital assets they hold. Storing funds on an exchange exposes them to potential security breaches, such as exchange hacks or insider attacks. If an exchange is compromised, there is a risk of losing your funds entirely. When you store funds on an exchange, you essentially transfer custody and control of your assets to the exchange. This means you are reliant on the exchange's security measures, operational practices, and overall trustworthiness. If the exchange experiences technical issues, goes offline, or engages in fraudulent activities, you may face difficulties accessing or recovering your funds. Cryptocurrency regulations vary across jurisdictions, and exchanges can sometimes face legal or regulatory challenges. In such cases, your funds might be subject to freezes, seizures, or delays due to regulatory actions against the exchange.

So where should you store your crypto?

Cold storage, which involves offline wallets, is considered one of the safest methods to store bitcoin. These wallets are not connected to the internet, reducing the risk of unauthorized access.

Hot wallets, although accessible online, are still convenient for certain users who require frequent access to their funds.

For the highest level of security, consider using a non-custodial cold hardware wallet to store your bitcoin and other cryptocurrencies in the long term.

Keep only the amount of cryptocurrency you intend to use in your hot wallet. After completing your transactions, it is advisable to transfer the remaining funds back to cold storage to minimize potential risks.

1. **Risk Management-** There is one thing that can change the entire scenario for a person engaging in cryptocurrency, this factor is risk management. No matter, if you are an expert at trading or a pro at investments, if you don't know how to manage your risk you can end up losing it all. Risk management can be best understood with the help of an example.

Let's consider an example of a person named Sara. Sara actively invests in cryptocurrency and has over the years learnt the importance of risk management. She analyzes before investing, she tracks before trading and she thinks before acting on her instincts. She has an objective discipline and does not run on her emotions while trading. Sara is a cryptocurrency trader who has learnt the importance of risk management through her experiences as well as education. Here's how she applies risk management strategies:

Sara understands the importance of diversifying her portfolio in order to mitigate risks. Instead of investing all her funds in a single cryptocurrency, she diversifies her investments across different coins, including Bitcoin (BTC), Ethereum (ETH), Ripple (XRP), and Cardano (ADA). By diversifying her holdings, she reduces the potential impact of a decline in any individual cryptocurrency. Her holdings can at best balance her loss in individual assets with profit or neutrality in the others.

Sara also keeps her risk appetite and risk tolerance in check. She measures them based on her financial goals and personal circumstances. She determines the amount of capital she is willing to allocate to cryptocurrencies and then invests accordingly a percentage of her overall investment portfolio in it. This helps her avoid overexposure to the highly volatile crypto market and still make use of the investment opportunity.

Sara follows a disciplined approach to position sizing. Before entering any trade, she carefully calculates the amount of capital she is willing to risk, considering factors such as the potential upside, downside, and her risk tolerance level. By determining the appropriate position size for each trade, she ensures that no single trade has an excessive impact on her overall portfolio.

Sara also uses stop-loss orders to protect her investments from significant losses. For example, when she enters a trade, she sets a stop-loss order at a predefined percentage below her entry point. If the price moves against that threshold, the stop-loss order triggers, automatically selling her position and limiting potential losses. She also employs take-profit orders to secure profits by automatically selling a portion of her holdings when a predefined profit target is reached.

Sara regularly takes initiative to learn about market trends, news, and developments in the cryptocurrency industry. She reads to understand more, researches, performs technical and fundamental analysis, and keeps track of any potential risks or events that could impact the market. This knowledge enables her to make informed decisions and adjust her strategies accordingly.

Lastly she trades with a fair understanding of trading psychology. She understands that emotions can negatively influence trading decisions. She strives to remain rational and avoids making impulsive trades driven by fear, greed, or FOMO. By maintaining emotional discipline, she can stick to her risk management plan and make objective decisions based on data and analysis.

On the contrary if a trader/investor doesn't manage his risk effectively they can suffer a great deal of loss as risk management is of utmost importance. In such case, a trader would do the following errors

Lack of Diversification

Trading without Stop loss

Emotional trading

Lack of research and analysis

Stakes the money that they are not ready to lose

1. Fundamental analysis of the project

I would mark this lesson as the most important one as it is one point which is of great use but is not discussed oftenly in the market. Fundamental analysis requires a lot of research and an in depth knowledge which is why it is usually shelved and not given much importance. However, it is the most crucial take away for a trader/investor. Cryptocurrencies are transparent financial systems. Every blockchain is backed by a particular type of technology. And its derivative coin runs on that particular technology. These blockchains have front end, back end, databases; many other technical aspects and applications. These applications generally are of two major types, one being, public and another private. Public applications are the ones that have open source code and are available for public viewership. Blockchain technology is called transparent because it comes under the open source application. Since blockchains are available in the public view, you can check each development, recent activity and history about the listed coins. You can check this information through repositories such as Github and Uniswap. These repositories provide databases of multiple projects, recording developments and codes. You can also check the contribution done by each developer and even check the changes made in the chain codes. The reason why I explained this is, in our conventional financial systems, there were relatively lesser transparencies and we needed to connect their significance and meaning through geopolitical and commercial movements. On the contrary with cryptocurrency and block chain technology, things are easier, more transparent and clearer to understand. So if the information is available why not make use of it and apply it to your benefit.

There are times when investors and traders leave their funds in isolation, without keeping updated with the progress on the invested project. This is when their investments begin to lose value. Consider this, if you acquire a skill and you shelve it without putting it into everyday use, it will become dormant in your memory in some time. Similarly the projects that were once promising might go redundant in absence of continuous progress. And sadly this is what has been happening to some of the coins and crypto projects lately. Why do you think people trust coins like Bitcoin and Ethereum more, investing huge amounts of money in them? It may be for new entrants that market sentiment drives their decision but for the market veterans, it is the trust in the white paper, in the transparency, in the advancements and the progress of Bitcoin, which drives more money into it by them.

In the previous chapters I have already discussed how to conduct fundamental analysis. You can take help from the manual and secure yourself from the projects that can be potential scams or worn out in capacities and ideas. Therefore it is always my advice to focus on the projects that are new, innovative and that strive towards a continuous developmental path. Don't hold these sit coins and waste your investment time on coins that are barely moving or progressing. One of the examples for this is TRON, people invested their money here hoping for a better growth but the coin has not moved for at least two alt seasons, no new version of it has been developed, encasing its investors for the time being. Most of the coins have jumped 2x, 3x, 4x, even 10x but what about the coins like ETN, XRP, TRX, BCN? They have not changed and are not undergoing any actual development. Code never lies and since these codes are openly available it is your duty to track them and reevaluate your holdings from time to time.

2. Right time to enter/exit

Before you begin to understand a strategy, try to understand the market. Before you try to understand the micro, try to understand the macro. It is the same thing when it comes to the market timing in cryptocurrency. People learn strategies first and then apply it everywhere without first analyzing the market conditions or market type. Market timing is about first understanding the market, the dynamism of cryptocurrency, then about learning the tools. If you don't know how to drive a car, you can't use strategies to enhance your learning. Strategies are application based and to master them you should first learn and then apply. Let's consider an example of Johnny. Johnny recently learned a strategy called "buying the dip" in the cryptocurrency market. The strategy underlines the basic principle that when the prices dip and when there is panic selling, one should buy the asset and then potentially gain profits when the price recovers. Johnny was excited to know and to assume that trading was just this simple principle and he began to apply this strategy to every cryptocurrency he came across. He did not study further and went on without considering other factors. One day, John heard about a new cryptocurrency called x Coin that had recently seen a price drop. Johnny, without conducting any research on the project, market conditions, or the reasons behind the price drop, immediately bought a large amount of x Coin. He continued to hold it in hope of a price recovery but unfortunately x Coin turned out to be a poorly designed project. There was very little real-world utility and the price continued to plummet even further. He failed to recognize that his knowledge was incomplete and that the strategy of buying the dip was not suitable for every cryptocurrency, especially those with fundamental issues.

However Johnny, undeterred by this initial setback, continued to apply the same strategy to other cryptocurrencies, expecting similar results. He failed to understand the diversity and dynamism of the cryptocurrency market, where each coin has its own unique characteristics, factors, and market conditions.

As a result, Johnny continued to buy into downtrends, getting caught in prolonged bear markets, and experiencing significant losses.

On some occasions this strategy did work but most of the times it did not, leading Johnny frustrated and confused. In this example, John's lack of understanding about when to apply the "buying the dip" strategy and his failure to consider other crucial factors in the cryptocurrency market led to poor decision-making and financial losses. It emphasizes the importance of learning multiple strategies, conducting thorough research, and understanding the nuances of different cryptocurrencies before applying any investment approach.

The reason why I mentioned Johnny's story is because most of the people want a straight answer to market timing, however the answer is not so simple. Crypto markets take different forms at different times. Sometimes there is a trending market and sometimes there is a sideways market. Both of the market stances work differently, require different strategies to position a correct entry and an exit. The main difference between a successful investor and a failed one is these two factors, entry and exit. If you buy something and hold it even when it has reached its peak price, you enter the greed circle which delays your exit and thus damages your profit. SImilarly if you buy at peak or at dips of a fundamentally weak coin, you create a wrong entry which also eats away your money.

Thus for a right entry and exit, you will need to know more than the simple principle of buy the dip and sell the top. However right these lines are, they do not apply everywhere and to all market stances.

3. Verify and check your exchange

It is my advice that whenever you see a new coin on an exchange platform, do not buy it at the top of its game. What happens is, when a platform enlists a coin initially it pumps its numbers. There have been reports where exchanges like Binance have listed certain coins which were unverified and were held by a group of minority owners. When people invest in these coins, they face problems linked to their movement and genuine price. When confronted, the CEOs' of these exchanges often wash their hands off responsibility, shifting the blame onto investors. Sometimes, the accounts linked to these exchanges are also hacked by third parties. In such cases too, the platform owners have been seen avoiding responsibility and stating that their platforms are not for parking funds but only for exchanging. In such scenarios it is very difficult to retrieve your funds or even register your grievance. Always check for deposit rates, liquidity terms, authenticity, founder details, among many other points to make sure that your money is safe on the platforms. Or else, choose only those platforms that are well known and are used by many people. High trading fees in the form of brokerage fees can significantly diminish your trading profits. To mitigate this, it is crucial to select a broker or exchange that provides low-fee trading options while ensuring high volume and liquidity.

Chapter 9

SEVEN mistakes

Why is it that 90% of the traders lose their money in the process of trading and investing? It's been a few years since I have been a part of the crypto market and I have seen a spectrum of trading behavioral patterns. These patterns range from that of a beginner to an expert. From someone who loses money to someone who has made millions with the same asset. As quoted before, 90% of the people who invest or trade in the market end up with a loss. Then what is it that separates the remaining 10% from the 90%. Before beginning to answer that question, I would like to bring to your notice the staking difference in the two percentages. It's a ninety percent of those who fail. This is not a small number rather something that signifies that 9 out of 10 people end up losing money in the investment that they were hoping to profit from. Over the years with whatever I have seen, learnt, experimented, errored and applied I have observed that there are some common mistakes that traders and investors tend to commit around crypto. These mistakes can be summed up into seven most common ones which if corrected can save you your money and if not can cost you whatever you have.

1. Lack of proper tools

Learning about a new concept is really exciting, especially if it comes along with some money. With cryptocurrency, there are channels everywhere, promising the right knowledge, right signals, right everything for you but the only stress is how to figure out what to learn and what to not. On the flip side, there are some beginners that do not consider the knowledge being imparted and they jump into the process without properly learning first. Lack of knowledge and proper tools thus become a limitation on these excited traders. They incur losses or limit their own potential of earning profits due to this reason.

Secondly, when I mention tools I do not mean that you should have multiple screens for tracking, high speed internet or hardware. I am talking about a proper plan and a set of knowledge-based strategies that you are going to use. Assume that you want to participate in a national athletics championship and in it you want to compete at racing. Also consider that you are not a born athlete and in order to reach the nationals you will have to start at the beginning. Running appears to be a simple task but running for a championship involves additional aspects which are much more complex than the version of running you are familiar with. In the process, you will learn various strategies, garner various tools, you might need help from a coach or support from a team and these will help you to achieve your goal. Also, you will not crack the nationals in one go, you will have to clear the intermediate stages that will help you reach the top. Similarly, trading and investing require a process based understanding. It is a skill that you are trying to master. It's like preparing to be an athlete, a singer, a dancer, or any other professional, you choose the skill, you learn about it and then you practice it to get better. When you begin to trade, first learn its basics, its fundamentals and then use the learnt knowledge for application. Tools also cover fundamental analysis of not just the asset but also of the platform where you are planning to trade or invest. Let me explain the cost of lacking such tools with an example.

Emily is a girl who had recently learnt about cryptocurrency. She didn't have much experience in finance or trading, but she was determined to make a quick profit. She opened an account on a popular crypto exchange platform and deposited a significant portion of her savings into it. Without understanding the basics, she started randomly buying and selling various cryptocurrencies based on tips she found on social media or from friends who claimed to be experts.

Instead of studying market trends, analyzing charts, and researching projects, Emily relied solely on luck and gut feelings. She believed that if she bought a cryptocurrency and held onto it for a short period, it would miraculously increase in value, granting her huge returns. She would often panic sell during market dips, fearing she would lose all her money, and then buy back at higher prices when the market started to recover.

As days turned into weeks and weeks into months, Emily's portfolio began to shrink. The lack of knowledge and proper trading strategies started taking its toll on her investments.

She made impulsive decisions, chasing "hot" coins without understanding their fundamentals or long-term prospects. Sometimes she even invested in fraudulent or questionable projects because they promised quick gains.

Emily's savings were dwindling rapidly, and she started experiencing sleepless nights filled with anxiety and regret. She realized that her haphazard approach to crypto trading was nothing more than gambling, and the odds were not in her favor. She finally understood that successful trading required knowledge, discipline, and a well-thought-out strategy. Overtime her philosophy and approach towards trading changed and she stopped gambling her money away.

2. Not cutting loss

Cutting your loss foremostly includes using stop loss and secondly exiting when your first incur a significant loss. Cutting your loss is mostly important for traders and since they engage in short term buying-selling, a small change in trends can also disturb their outputs. In this case it is very important to use stop loss and timely exit from the market. I have seen some people who let their funds slide down even when they are up frontly witnessing the downtrend in the market, just in the hope of a price recovery. Sometimes hope and prays can help you out but this is rarely the case of a volatile market like crypto. Let's understand this mistake with an example.

Let's take a look at the story of Raj, an Indian trader who was a lot into trading but never considered the importance of cutting his losses. This mistake ultimately led to significant financial losses for him.

Raj was an enthusiastic and confident trader who had

been actively involved in the cryptocurrency market for several years. He had experienced some initial success, making substantial profits by riding the upward trends of various cryptocurrencies. However, Raj had a deeply ingrained belief that he didn't need to cut his losses when a trade was going against him. He firmly believed that the market would eventually turn in his favor, and he would be able to recoup his losses.

One day, Raj came across a new altcoin that he believed had great potential. Without conducting thorough research or analyzing the project's fundamentals, he invested a substantial amount of his capital into it. Initially, the market responded positively, and the price of the altcoin started to rise, reinforcing Raj's confidence in his investment.

However, as time went on, the market sentiment shifted, and the altcoin's value began to decline rapidly. Instead of cutting his losses and accepting that he had made a wrong investment, Raj held onto his position, convinced that a rebound was just around the corner. As the price continued to drop, Raj started losing a significant portion of his invested capital.

Despite warnings from fellow traders and market indicators signaling a further decline, Raj remained stubborn, refusing to sell at a loss. He believed that his perseverance and trust in the project would eventually pay off. Unfortunately, the altcoin continued its downward spiral, wiping out a significant portion of Raj's portfolio.

As the losses mounted, Raj found himself in a difficult situation. He was emotionally attached to the investment, holding onto the hope of recovering his losses. His unwillingness to cut his losses resulted in a substantial financial setback, and he was unable to salvage his investment or protect his capital.

Ultimately, Raj's failure to cut his losses was a costly mistake. The altcoin he invested in eventually became virtually worthless, erasing a significant portion of his trading account. Had Raj adopted a more disciplined approach and implemented a stop-loss strategy, he could have limited his losses and preserved his capital for other trading opportunities.

This example highlights the importance of setting predefined stop-loss levels and having a clear risk management strategy in cryptocurrency trading. Cutting losses is an essential part of trading to prevent substantial financial damage. Without a willingness to accept losses and exit losing trades, traders like Raj can find themselves in dire situations, unable to recover financially from poor investment decisions.

3. Not having a trading plan

This is a mistake especially common in beginners. A trading plan helps you to strategize and calculate before things go right or even wrong. MOst of the people in life only choose to see the positive side of things. They choose to consciously ignore or subdue the possibilities of something negative that might happen. Trading is no different for these people. When you invest your money, you should evaluate both sides of the trade, evaluate the positive and the negative, profit and loss. However, as I said, most traders prepare for a profit, for a boom but they never prepare for loss, for the time when their investments might turn into nothing. This is a colossal mistake as it blinds you from preparing and cushioning yourself against an unwanted event. When you don't evaluate the full picture, you do not study well, you do not research well into the entire picture. Your market timings, entry exit plans, stop loss, tools, strategies nothing is even brought to picture if you do not plan things out. Our mind seldom understands a puzzled scenario, it is us who need to bring clarity by piecing together the parts and making a picture that is easy to decipher by our brains. In absence of this clarity, our brain remains confused, not being able to focus and unable to create a better output.

Here's an example of a man named Raj who wants to trade but lacks a structured plan and relies on impulsive decision-making:

Raj, a 35-year-old software engineer, developed an interest in trading and decided to try his hand at the financial markets. However, he approached trading with a haphazard mindset, lacking a well-defined plan or strategy. Raj would often rely on high adrenaline and rushes of excitement, making impulsive trading decisions without thorough evaluation and analysis.

Whenever Raj observed a sudden surge in a particular stock or market, he would jump in without conducting proper research. He would disregard important indicators, such as market trends, fundamental analysis, and risk management principles. Raj would make trading decisions purely based on gut feelings or the desire to experience the thrill of a volatile market.

As a result, Raj experienced mixed outcomes. Sometimes his impulsive trades would lead to short-term gains, which further fueled his excitement. However, more often than not, his lack of evaluation and analysis would result in losses, causing frustration and disappointment.

Over time, Raj began to realize the shortcomings of his approach. He understood that successful trading required a structured plan, discipline, and a thorough understanding of market dynamics. Recognizing the importance of education and preparation, Raj decided to rectify his approach.

Raj started studying trading strategies, market analysis techniques, and risk management principles. He immersed himself in books, online courses, and educational resources to gain a deeper understanding of the financial markets. He learned about technical analysis, fundamental analysis, and various indicators that could help him make informed trading decisions.

With his newfound knowledge, Raj developed a trading plan that included specific entry and exit criteria, risk management guidelines, and a focus on long-term profitability rather than short-term excitement. He adopted a more patient approach, waiting for favorable setups and conducting thorough analysis before entering any trades.

As Raj implemented his structured trading plan, he noticed a significant improvement in his trading results. By relying on careful evaluation and analysis, he reduced impulsive trades and made more informed decisions. He also managed risk more effectively, minimizing losses and increasing his overall profitability.

Raj's transformation serves as a reminder of the importance of having a well-defined plan and the discipline to adhere to it. By shifting from impulsive trading to a structured approach, he was able to improve his trading outcomes and set himself up for long-term success in the financial markets.

4. Following others blindly

As I said before there are many channels out there who are talking about cryptocurrency. Some are useful and credible while some not so much. In a world full of information there is an equally powerful world of misinformation. For example, if you are learning to cook, beginning from scratch, you should always find new ways better ways and more convenient ways to learn about it. But at the very least, no matter how unskilled you are at it, you know about your preferred taste, your preferred base, whether you are a vegetarian or a non-vegetarian. You know all this even though you don't know much about cooking. Similarly while searching through these knowledge avenues, you at least know your risk appetite, legal-illegal, good-bad(at least for you).

And as you progress you will begin to understand a few things more, where you should begin to corroborate the technical advice through your research as well. For instance if someone advises you to buy stocks of tesla because they predict a future boom in the same, your job is to find out if there is any substance to this assumption. If Tesla is launching something new, or creating something new, anything that can provide solid grounds to this prediction. Without that no matter who the person is, even if it is me, you should never choose to blindly accept the signals or advises.

Here's an example of an Indian boy named Rahul who followed advice from others blindly and invested his money in crypto assets:

Rahul, a 22-year-old college student from Mumbai, had recently heard about the growing popularity of cryptocurrencies like Bitcoin and Ethereum. Intrigued by the potential for high returns, he decided to invest his hard-earned savings of ₹50,000 ($700) in the crypto market. However, Rahul had no prior experience or knowledge of investing in cryptocurrencies.

One day, Rahul overheard a conversation between his classmates, Aman and Neha, who were discussing their recent success in crypto investments. Aman claimed to have made substantial profits by following a particular strategy, and Neha endorsed his claims, saying she had also seen impressive returns.

Excited by their conversation, Rahul approached Aman and Neha, seeking guidance on how to invest in cryptocurrencies. Both of them were happy to help and shared their strategies and recommendations with him. They suggested specific coins and advised Rahul to invest a significant portion of his savings into those particular assets.

Without conducting any further research or seeking additional opinions, Rahul blindly followed their advice and invested all of his ₹50,000 in those recommended cryptocurrencies. He believed that since Aman and Neha had experienced success, their advice would surely lead to similar results for him.

Unfortunately, the crypto market turned highly volatile shortly after Rahul's investment. The prices of the recommended coins plummeted due to various market factors, and Rahul's investment took a significant hit. He watched as his portfolio value diminished rapidly, leaving him in a state of panic and regret.

Realizing the consequences of his impulsive decision, Rahul understood the importance of conducting thorough research and seeking professional advice before making any investment. He recognized that blindly following advice from others, without understanding the underlying risks and dynamics, could lead to undesirable outcomes.

This experience served as a valuable lesson for Rahul. He decided to educate himself on investing principles, market trends, and risk management strategies. Rahul also sought guidance from financial advisors and professionals to make informed investment decisions in the future. By learning from his mistake, he transformed his initial setback into an opportunity to become a more knowledgeable and cautious investor.

5. Going too big = overtrade

I always say that invest only that chunk of money into trading which you would be okay with losing. I can understand that when there is a prospect of earning more, you would want to put in more. This ideology is in line with how we see things around us. When you want something big, you put in the required efforts, you work hard and put in more hours, intelligence into it. However, in trading investing more doesn't always mean you'll earn more. It is unlike other situations in life. With more investment, you need more caution, more knowledge and more experience.

Here's an example of a girl named Priya who had limited knowledge about trading in cryptocurrency but experienced initial success followed by a significant loss:

Priya, a 25-year-old software engineer from Bengaluru, became intrigued by the potential of making money through cryptocurrency trading. Despite her limited understanding of the market dynamics, she decided to invest a small sum of ₹10,000 ($140) in Bitcoin.

To her surprise, within a short period, the value of Bitcoin soared, and Priya found herself with ₹20,000 ($280) in her trading account. Encouraged by her initial success and unaware of the potential risks, Priya decided to reinvest her entire principal along with the profit she had earned.

With ₹20,000 ($280) as her new starting capital, Priya entered the market once again. This time, she experienced an even greater profit, witnessing her account balance rise to ₹100,000 ($1,400). Although she was thrilled with her results, she was still trading without a solid understanding of the market and relying mostly on luck.

Feeling emboldened by her success, Priya decided to take a bigger risk. Without considering the potential consequences, she invested ₹1,000,000 ($14,000), which was ten times her initial sum, into cryptocurrency trading. Unfortunately, this time the market took a downturn, and Priya ended up incurring a loss. Her account balance dwindled, leaving her with only ₹800,000 ($11,200).

The loss served as a wake-up call for Priya, who realized the importance of knowledge and experience in trading. She understood that her initial success was mostly due to fortunate timing and market conditions rather than her own skills. Determined to make better decisions, she committed herself to learn about cryptocurrency trading and gain a deeper understanding of market analysis, risk management, and trading strategies.

Priya sought out educational resources, attended

webinars, and joined online communities of experienced traders. She started following market trends, analyzing charts, and keeping up with news that impacted the cryptocurrency market. Slowly but steadily, Priya built her knowledge and trading expertise.

Recognizing the importance of managing risk, Priya adopted a more cautious approach. She diversified her investment portfolio, set clear profit targets, and established stop-loss orders to limit potential losses. Over time, with diligent research, strategic decision-making, and risk management, Priya was able to regain her losses and generate consistent profits from her cryptocurrency trades.

Priya's journey taught her a valuable lesson about the significance of education, experience, and calculated decision-making in the world of cryptocurrency trading. She became a more knowledgeable and prudent trader, using her initial setbacks as stepping stones towards long-term success.

6. Panic buying and selling

Some two years ago there was a wave of anticipation running on the possible ban on cryptocurrency. The whole market around this time was experiencing panic selling based on the uncertain future of their assets. Caught in these currents were also people who not only sold their bitcoins and other assets on losing margins but also sold stable coins like USDT just because they went into the panic mode. But what happened after that, cryptocurrency was not banned but only brought under a heavier taxation bracket.

Here's an example of a boy named Arjun who was

trading during uncertain times regarding the future of cryptocurrency in Indian law:

Arjun, a 28-year-old entrepreneur from Delhi, had been actively trading cryptocurrencies for several years. He had experienced both ups and downs in the market but remained optimistic about the potential of digital assets. However, during this period, the Indian government started expressing concerns about the unregulated nature of cryptocurrencies and hinted at the possibility of imposing stricter regulations or even a ban.

As news of the uncertain regulatory landscape spread, panic swept through the crypto community in India. Many traders, including Arjun, began to worry about the future of their investments. Arjun's portfolio, which had been performing well until then, started to lose value amidst the growing uncertainty.

Unable to handle the mounting pressure and fearing a potential ban on cryptocurrencies, Arjun made a hasty decision. Without waiting for any official judgment or clarity from the government, he sold off his entire cryptocurrency holdings in a state of panic. He assumed that the worst-case scenario of a complete ban was imminent and wanted to minimize his potential losses.

However, shortly after Arjun sold his cryptocurrencies, the Indian government clarified its stance on cryptocurrencies. Instead of imposing a complete ban, they opted for stricter regulations to monitor the crypto market. This unexpected turn of events caught Arjun off guard. He realized that he had made a big mistake by acting out of fear and assuming the worst without waiting for the official announcement.

As the regulatory picture became clearer, the market began to stabilize, and cryptocurrencies started to recover from the initial panic-induced sell-off. Arjun witnessed the value of the cryptocurrencies he had sold rise significantly, missing out on potential profits.

Arjun learned a valuable lesson about the importance of patience, research, and not making impulsive decisions based on assumptions or rumors. He understood that it was essential to wait for official announcements and gather accurate information before taking any significant actions regarding his investments.

Motivated by his mistake, Arjun decided to enhance his knowledge about the crypto market, regulatory developments, and risk management strategies. He closely followed updates from reliable sources and sought guidance from industry experts to make informed decisions in the future.

Although Arjun incurred a loss due to his panic-driven selling, he recognized the value of learning from his mistakes. With a more cautious and informed approach, he resumed his cryptocurrency trading activities, determined to navigate the regulatory landscape more effectively and make prudent investment decisions.

7. Placing earning before learning

You know what is the most common context of emails that I receive? It is people asking me to advise upon the name of the coin to invest in, a coin that can get them a profit of 2x , 3x , 10x.And I do not usually see people seeking advice on where could they find lessons on fundamental and technical analysis, what are the latest tools they could use, nothing of this sort. This I say is a classic example of putting earning before learning.

Consider this, when an army personnel is under training, they are put through much worse than what they might actually witness during their serving period. But the preparation is such that it prepares them for any unforeseen circumstances. Army, navy or any other defense force they go by the simple rule, if you can't survive training, you can't survive the reality too. Similarly before earning I would say

1. Start with paper money instead of real money
2. Learn basics first
3. Further your knowledge by learning tools and strategies
4. Choose your own style and don't follow others blindly
5. Maintain a trading journal
6. Follow the related news regularly and stay up to date
7. Practice and keep upgrading

Lastly I would say don't just rely on others for investing advice. You are investing for yourself, with your money, for your own goals, why should you ask others about how to achieve that. If you wish to seek advice, do that in terms of learning the fundamentals. Do that in a way that you are moving towards becoming independent in approach. You learn from others so that you can one day be self reliant, you don't ask from others to be your advising crutch for the rest of your life.

Here's an example of a person named Ankit who invested his money without learning, without preparing for the consequences, and relied heavily on others for investment advice:

Ankit, a 30-year-old marketing professional, became intrigued by the world of cryptocurrencies after hearing stories of people making significant profits. Excited by the potential financial gains, Ankit decided to invest a substantial sum of money without taking the time to learn about the basics of investing or preparing for the potential consequences.

Instead of educating himself about the cryptocurrency market, Ankit relied heavily on others for investment advice. He would eagerly search for online forums, social media groups, and influencers who claimed to have insider knowledge about the "next big thing" in cryptocurrencies. Ankit would blindly follow their recommendations without conducting any independent research or evaluating the risks involved.

As a result, Ankit's investment journey became a series of impulsive decisions based on the advice of others. He constantly sought out opinions on what coins to buy, when to buy, and when to sell. Ankit lacked a thorough understanding of the market dynamics, didn't consider his risk tolerance, and failed to prepare for potential losses.

Unfortunately, Ankit's lack of preparation and reliance on others led to unfavorable outcomes. He experienced a rollercoaster of gains and losses, often falling victim to market volatility and poor investment choices. When the market turned bearish, Ankit found himself in a state of panic, uncertain about what actions to take or how to protect his capital.

Realizing the flaws in his approach, Ankit understood the importance of personal responsibility and learning from his mistakes. He recognized that investing without proper education and understanding the risks involved could lead to financial losses and emotional distress.

Determined to change his approach, Ankit decided to educate himself about investing and cryptocurrencies. He began by learning the fundamentals of investing, risk management techniques, and conducting in-depth research on various coins and projects. He also sought guidance from reputable sources and consulted financial advisors to gain a better understanding of the market.

As Ankit developed a solid foundation of knowledge, he started to make more informed investment decisions. He diversified his portfolio, set realistic expectations, and adopted a long-term investment strategy. Ankit accepted the inherent risks of the market and prepared himself mentally and financially to face the consequences of his investments.

Over time, Ankit's newfound approach led to more consistent results. While he still experienced fluctuations in the market, his informed decisions and commitment to learning helped him navigate the complexities of the cryptocurrency world more effectively.

Ankit's journey serves as a lesson about the importance of personal responsibility, education, and independent research when it comes to investing. By taking charge of his financial decisions and understanding the risks involved, Ankit transformed himself into a more knowledgeable and empowered investor.

Chapter 10

The Past, Present and Future of cryptocurrency

PAST-

Satoshi Nakamoto, in 2009 created a unique digital currency with no physical counterparts, called Bitcoin. The person/people behind this name still remain anonymous, with certain speculations of his true identity in the market but with no substantial luck. Some people connect this to the cyber punk revolution for the decentralized internet. The "Cyberpunks Revolution of Cryptocurrency" refers to a combination where the cyberpunk movement found its expression through the rise of cryptocurrencies. The cyberpunk genre, popularized in science fiction literature and films, displays a dystopian future where advanced technology, computer hacking, and societal rebellion play prominent roles.

The genre talks about the importance of the ideals of decentralization, privacy, and digital freedom. These ideals found their best expression through the inherent nature of cryptocurrencies, they were decentralized, away from the control of any one central authority, echoing the rebellious spirit of cyberpunk narratives.

These individuals, often self-proclaimed "cypherpunks," advocate for the use of cryptography, encryption, and blockchain technology to empower individuals, challenge centralized authorities, and create alternative financial systems. They stand for the right to privacy and the need to eliminate a power structure that needs all their information to validate financial transactions. They believe in the potential of cryptocurrencies to reshape this traditional power structures, bypass intermediaries, and enable greater financial inclusivity.

The cyberpunks revolution of cryptocurrency can be seen in various aspects:

1. **Decentralization:** Cyberpunks emphasize the importance of decentralized systems, where no single authority or institution has control over the network or the currency. They support cryptocurrencies that operate on decentralized blockchains, such as Bitcoin or Ethereum, as opposed to centralized digital currencies issued by governments or financial institutions.

2. **Privacy and Anonymity:** In line with cyberpunk ideology, privacy is a key focus for cyberpunks involved in cryptocurrencies. They advocate for privacy-enhancing technologies, such as anonymous transactions or privacy coins, that provide individuals with greater control over their personal and financial information.

3. **Anti-establishment Stance:** Cyberpunks often challenge traditional financial institutions and government control over money. They view cryptocurrencies as a means to disrupt established financial systems and promote a more equitable and open society.

4. **Technology Empowerment:** The cyberpunks revolution of cryptocurrency embraces the use of technology, cryptography, and blockchain as tools for empowerment. They believe that these technologies can help individuals regain control over their financial lives and challenge existing power structures.

PRESENT-

Cryptocurrencies were thought of as a revolution which would change the financial systems down the line. It's been around 15 years since the first cryptocurrency and with 56 different countries worldwide adopting the new currency, cryptos have changed in form, vision and use case. Cryptos came with the Idea of decentralization and replacement of the traditional financial systems. However over the years it was observed that cryptos were adopted more in the places where traditional systems faltered. For example, in Countries like Argentina with hyper inflation and problematic currencies, cryptos were more readily used. On the contrary in countries like India, which have developed a cost-free digital transaction system, cryptos were not used for usual transactions. Ownership of digital currencies in Turkey was the highest in the world at 27.1% followed by Argentina at 23.5% -- well above global crypto ownership rate estimated at 11.9% -- according to data from research firm GWI. Whereas only 7.3% of the world's biggest population owns digital currency, according to the UN. Consumers from countries in Africa, Asia, and South America were most likely to be an owner of cryptocurrencies, such as Bitcoin, in 2023.

Is Cryptocurrency a Daily Utility or an Investment Tool?

The survey inquired about whether consumers owned or utilized cryptocurrencies, without specifying their specific usage or purpose. Certain countries, however, exhibit a higher tendency to employ digital currencies for everyday transactions. For instance, Nigeria has increasingly embraced mobile money operations for in-store payments and remittances to family and friends. In 2019, Polish consumers had the option to purchase various products using cryptocurrencies. On the contrary, Vietnam strictly prohibits the use of Bitcoin and other cryptocurrencies as payment methods, although owning cryptocurrencies as an investment is permissible.

Which countries are more inclined towards cryptocurrency investments?

A survey conducted in early 2020 revealed that professional investors seeking cryptocurrency-themed ETFs were more prevalent in Europe compared to the United States or China. In 2020, a majority of the largest crypto hedge fund managers in Europe were based in the United Kingdom and Switzerland, with Switzerland boasting the highest cryptocurrency adoption rate in Europe, as per Statista's Global Consumer Survey. Whether there have been any changes to this scenario since 2021 remains uncertain.

Are we really running on a revolution with cryptocurrency?

There are over 20,000 cryptocurrencies at present. All running on different use cases, different goals, different system but all together they are backed up by blockchain technology. In India as well, the goal is to make use of the revolutionizing block chain technology and there is not so much authority enthusiasm regarding the currencies themselves. So to answer this question, we are riding a revolution but the revolution is not of cryptocurrency or financial systems alone, we are riding a revolution that is based on the technology of blockchain. And this revolution is what we are calling WEB3. A world of internet where the ownership, privacy and authority will change forever.

Web3 and blockchain technology are closely intertwined, with blockchain serving as the underlying infrastructure that powers the decentralized and trustless nature of Web3 applications. By leveraging blockchain technology, Web3 aims to reshape various industries, including finance, governance, supply chain, healthcare, and more, by enabling new models of interaction, collaboration, and value exchange.

Blockchain technology forms the foundation of Web3 by providing the decentralized and immutable ledger that enables trust, transparency, and security in the digital realm. Web3 applications and platforms utilize blockchain networks to store and manage data, execute smart contracts, and enable peer-to-peer transactions without the need for intermediaries.

With Web3, users have greater control over their data and digital assets, as well as enhanced privacy and security.

Blockchain technology enables Web3 applications to operate in a decentralized manner, ensuring that no central authority or single point of failure has control over the network. This decentralized nature makes Web3 resistant to censorship and manipulation.

Thus the way forward for crypto would be building something bigger than what already is the idea of cryptocurrency.

FUTURE-

What is the future of cryptocurrency?

The answer to this again takes us back to the core technology which is Blockchain. Blockchain is a decentralized system and with no centralized authority, there is no central responsibility as well. Blockchain are transparent and accessible. In such case data and privacy become the center stage of concerns. Although crypted, the information on these chains can still be used by hackers and in case of such an attack, there is no one to solve it. Thus if the technology creators and propagators can bake unparalleled security into the core of the system, making it immune to hacking and other attacks, crypto's future might not remain in finance at all. It may expand to the whole iterations of the internet in the coming years.

The advent of cryptocurrency was epochal and it is continuing to change the course of our futures as well. Technology is dynamic in nature and it continues to develop with time. The similar case is with crypto as well. It is not even close its ideal form as of now but it holds the potential to craft a tomorrow that we have not imagined of.

On one end there are people, businesses, organization opening their doors for cryptocurrencies while on the other countries are closing up at the digital currency. At one end of spectrum you see Increased Mainstream Adoption, acceptance and recognition. More businesses, financial institutions, and individuals adopting and integrating cryptocurrencies into their operations. In response to this Governments and regulatory bodies around the world are working to develop frameworks to govern cryptocurrencies hoping that clear regulations may provide legal clarity and security, potentially encouraging more institutional investors and traditional financial institutions to enter the market.

Several central banks are exploring the concept of issuing their own digital currencies. This is also the case of India, where RBI may create its own cryptocurrency. These CBDCs could coexist with traditional cryptocurrencies or even serve as a potential competitor. CBDCs may offer the advantages of digital currencies while being backed and regulated by central banks.

This integration of cryptocurrencies into traditional financial systems will be an ongoing process. More financial institutions are offering cryptocurrency-related services, such as custodial solutions, trading platforms, and investment products. The bridging of traditional finance and cryptocurrencies could lead to increased liquidity and accessibility for digital assets.

We will also have to wait to see how the underlying technology of cryptocurrencies, blockchain, will continue to evolve and find use cases in other spheres of our lives. Improvements in scalability, privacy, and interoperability can enhance the functionality and usability of cryptocurrencies, making them more viable for everyday transactions and applications beyond finance.

Another thing that can happen is the advent of Stablecoins, which are cryptocurrencies pegged to stable assets like fiat currencies, offer stability and reduced volatility. These digital assets could potentially bridge the gap between traditional finance and cryptocurrencies by providing a stable medium of exchange and store of value.

Decentralized Finance (DeFi) has emerged as a prominent use case for cryptocurrencies, enabling various financial services like lending, borrowing, and trading without intermediaries. The growth of DeFi highlights the potential for decentralized applications and smart contracts to revolutionize traditional financial systems.

At present Is cryptocurrency legal in India?

This book has been written in the year 2023 and the following are the changes and developments that have taken place around crypto in India. Cryptocurrencies have been a topic of debate when it comes to their legal status in India. The government and the Reserve Bank of India (RBI) have not officially recognized them, leaving the matter in a state of uncertainty.

In April 2018, the RBI issued a circular expressing concerns about cryptocurrencies and their potential risks related to consumer protection, money laundering, and market integrity. This circular effectively prohibited citizens from dealing in cryptocurrencies. However, in a landmark case in 2020, the Supreme Court overturned this circular. The court favored the use of virtual currencies and suggested that they should be regulated by the RBI. The court acknowledged the RBI's right to protect public money but also indicated that alternatives to a complete ban must be explored.

Following the court's judgment, the government planned to introduce "The Cryptocurrency and Regulation of Official Digital Currency Bill, 2021" in Parliament. The proposed bill aimed to create a framework for an official digital currency issued by the RBI while prohibiting private cryptocurrencies, with certain exceptions to promote the underlying technology. However, the bill has not yet been introduced due to various complexities.

Despite the lack of clear regulations, the government has taken steps to monitor and regulate the cryptocurrency market. Amendments to the Companies Act in 2021 require companies to disclose their cryptocurrency investments and any associated profits or losses. Individuals holding virtual currencies are also required to provide details about their holdings and transactions.

The current state of cryptocurrency in India remains uncertain. While they are not considered legal tender, the government has also stated that they are not illegal. This ambiguity leaves the status of cryptocurrencies in a gray area in the country.

Chapter 11

Crypto through my eyes

So, we are towards the end of this book and till now we have discussed all the aspects and concepts of crypto trading. In this chapter, we will be summarizing whatever I have written till now, through practical application. I have prepared a case study for you, with Bitcoin through which you can understand even further as to how to apply what has been taught.

I have certain regulars and irregularities when it comes to my style of investing. As I have mentioned above as well, no matter if you are a beginner or an expert or somewhere in between, try to build your own unique style of going around with cryptocurrency. We invest or trade because we want to achieve a goal with that activity and our goals have causes. Similarly we all don't have the same capital, same resources, same time availability etc. If you have 50,000 INR to invest, the other person might only have 1000 INR. If one wants to become a crypto millionaire, the other might just want to experiment or diversify his portfolio. And for someone it might just be a hobby. So, before doing anything, find out your goal and your cause. Both are the vitals that drive human actions.

So let's start with the step by step process.

Step 1- Let's start with the basics

The first thing I do is I open CoinMarketCap. CoinMarketCap is a website that contains repositories of almost all of the coins in the market. Here you can find information, past, present and future trends of the coin; and also compare the assets with each other. It serves as a comprehensive platform for tracking the market capitalization, prices, trading volumes, and other key metrics of thousands of cryptocurrencies. CoinMarketCap aggregates data from different exchanges and presents it in a user-friendly manner, allowing users to quickly access and compare the performance of different cryptocurrencies.

The website provides real-time and historical data, enabling users to monitor the latest price movements, market trends, and overall market capitalization of the cryptocurrency industry. In addition to these features such as charts, portfolio tracking, news updates, and educational resources help users to stay informed and make informed investment decisions.

Step 2- Checklist-1

The next thing is to check ranks of the coins and to check their respective market caps. As I explained earlier, market cap is like those different land holding of each family member. It is the portion of the market capital that is held by that coin. I sort the possible coins based on their market cap and rankings. If a coin scores good on both these parameters, it means it is worth investing in. If a coin does not score good on these, it is better to stay away from them. So, ranking and market cap are like my first set of filters.

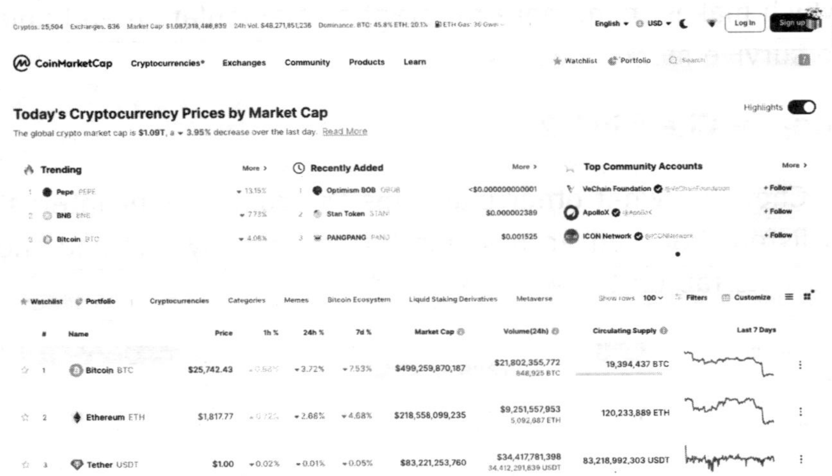

For instance, this picture shows the total market cap at this particular time to be $1.09Trillion. This is the total capitalization held by all the cryptocurrency that is present in existence(the ones that are authentically listed worldwide). Bitcoin carries approx. $4.9 Billion of market cap. This is a significant share of the market held by Bitcoin. Such an enormous market cap signifies that even if the market crashes or in case of unforeseen events, Bitcoin will offer some security and cushioning against the negative event. It's like if another pandemic hits our world, companies like TATA will offer more cushion against the negative market sentiment than any company which has a very low market cap. Purchasing a cryptocurrency with a high market capitalization shows that cryptocurrencies are widely used and accepted, which also positively affects their liquidity and stability. Large market cap coins often have stronger communities and better infrastructure, providing a robust ecosystem for investors. Additionally, a larger market capitalization may draw institutional investors, which might result in a higher rate of price growth. Cryptocurrencies with a higher market value also often have more visibility, which makes them more resistant to manipulation and able to survive market swings.

Step 3- Checklist-2

Check on what other platforms the coin of your interest is listed. You can access this information by opening the markets tab on the website.

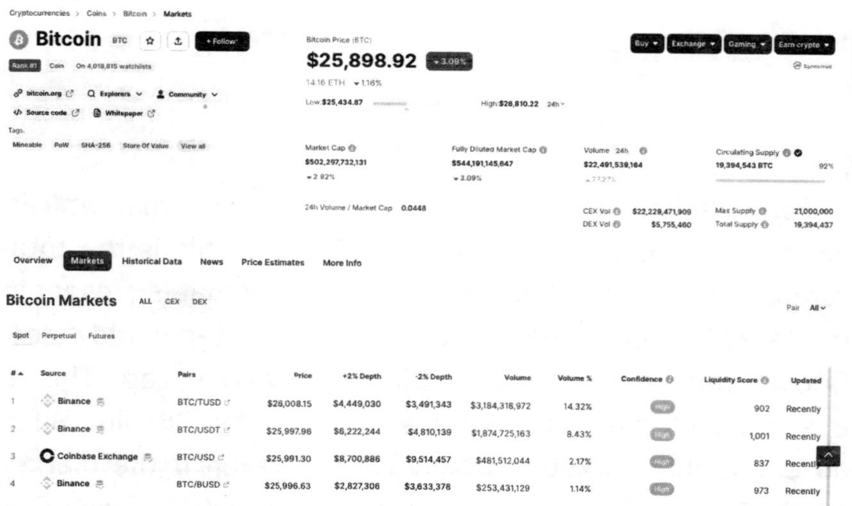

If you study Bitcoin, you can see that it is listed on around 100 other exchanges and is also listed on world's top 5 crypto exchange platforms, including Binance, Coinbase and KuCoin. Whereas if you perform the same analysis on Moss coin, another cryptocurrency, you will see that it is listed on only 2 exchanges and none of them are the ones that widely known or even the top 10 in the market.

You can then learn the overview on coin market cap but if still you want to learn further explore their website

Step 4- Find out more

Go a little further on the fundamental analysis. Begin the analysis with this understanding that each cryptocurrency is created to solve a problem.

a. First try to understand what is the problem that the coin of your interest is trying to solve. If you think that the proposed solution has a potential to create something big, you can clear it for the next stage of evaluation. For example ethereum is a fairly popular cryptocurrency. It was by Vitalik Buterin, to solve those problems which were left unsolved by Bitcoin. Ethereum is like a computer network that helps people create special programs called smart contracts. These smart contracts can do things like automatically transfer money or assets without needing a middleman. Ethereum wants to make it easier for developers to create these programs and for different programs to work together smoothly. It also wants to make the network faster and use less energy. The goal is to give people more control and make things work better in the world of digital applications. This vision has a strong use case for the future and is a genuine solution to a genuine problem. Thus, Ethereum can be promoted to the next stage of analysis.

b. **Market sentiment-** Market sentiment can be judged by using information from social media platforms, newspapers and conversations around cryptocurrency in the market. You can also make use of Fear and greed indexes that are available in the market that gives information about what is the sentiment around the coin in the market.

c. **Study the developer activity on the project** - A project that is working in isolation of any advancements should never be invested in. Take for instance coins like Bitcoin, Ethereum, they undergo continuous development in terms of their coding structure, signifying a continuous improvement and movement towards advancement. As I told your before, cryptocurrencies are open source code structures and they undergo recurrent developer actions on their codes. This activity can be easily monitored by using a tool called GitHub. GitHub is a website that can be used to see threads of developer activity on different cryptocurrencies. As mentioned above, if the development is active it means that even the backend of that coin is actively involved in progressing its existence. However if the development is not so active, it can signal that the project has failed to drive backend support from the developer community and is not lucrative enough in terms of vision and technology. Continuous activity also signifies the efficiency of issue resolution in the project. If there is a noted error, how long does it take for it to be resolved can all be seen in the timeline. And the more time it takes, the worse it says about the project efficiency.

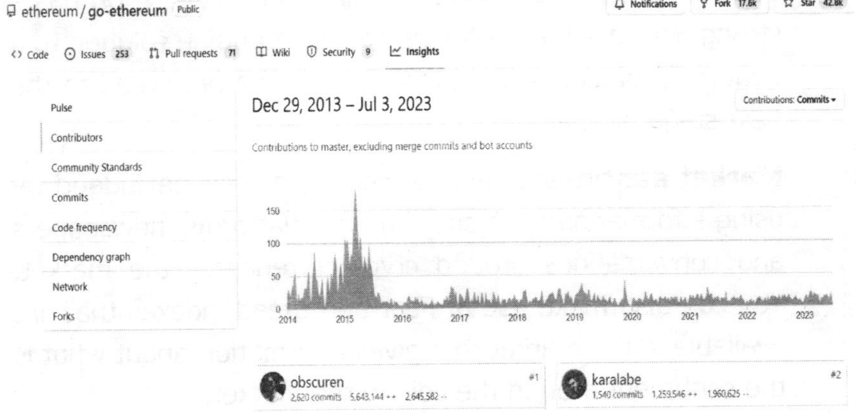

Once you complete fundamental analysis the next step is to analyze the coin from a technical perspective. During the analysis, we will use some quantitative tools like charts, lines etc.

I will give you an example of technical analysis by using one indicator that is Moving average.

Step 5- Study the numbers

For technical analysis go to trackingview.ai

Select the coin you want to analyze. Select the indicator as 'Moving average', now MA is also of three types, Simple, Exponential and weighted. For now you can use simple or exponential.

While performing technical analysis one must consider the example of gold in our everyday lives. Gold is an asset that Indians prefer to invest in. This preference increases manifold times especially during festivals. Festivals like Diwali are synonyms with the practice of buying and investing in Gold. The heightened demand pushes the gold prices and hence becomes a trend. Thus each year during Diwali, you can anticipate that the gold price will rise. The same is what is trend spotting is all about. To calculate and understand these trends, an asset's past performance is studied. This past activity is stored as data in charts and that is why these charts are used while performing technical analysis. When we spot a trend, it is always advised to confirm that trend with the help of tools that are available. These tools are called indicators. Multiple tools shall always be used for confirmation, as no single indicator can create the full picture.

Step 6- Use the indicators

I am going to explain with example two of my favourite indicators. One is the moving average and the other is the volume indicator (a custom indicator made by me).

Select moving average as the indicator and then configure the settings to plot lines according to your requirements. Moving averages can be studied using four lines. The length is from 20 days, 50 days, 100 days to 200 days.

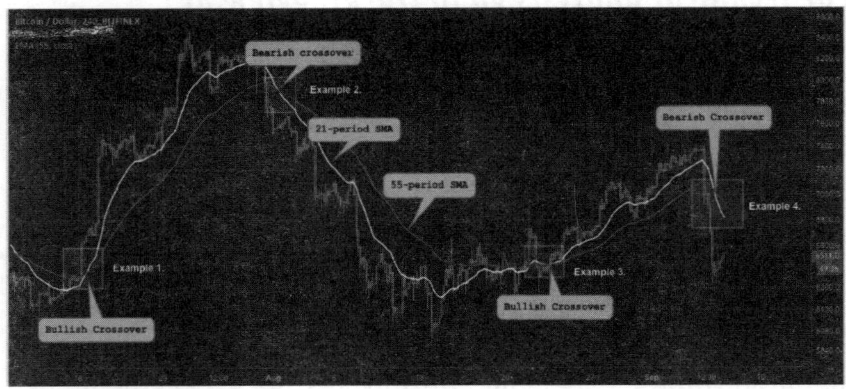

In the beginning you can use just two lines to study the chart and use closer time averages. For example, here there are 21 days and 55 days lines plotted. When the short day average line crosses over the long day average line, it leads to a bullish trend and when the short days average line crosses under the long day average line, it creates bearish market. The blue line here represents 21 days SMA or the short day average line. The red is of 55 days SMA and is long day average line. On very rare occasions a golden cross and a death cross can also occur. These are rare events that occur when a shorter-term moving average (such as the 50-day moving average) crosses above a longer-term moving average (such as the 200-day moving average) on a price chart. This event is considered bullish and is often interpreted as a positive signal for future price movements. It suggests that the asset's upward momentum may continue, potentially indicating a trend reversal or the start of an upward trend. Traders and investors often pay attention to golden crosses as they can influence buying and selling decisions. Death cross occurs when a shorter-term moving average (such as the 50-day moving average) crosses below a longer-term moving average (such as the 200-day moving average) on a price chart. The death cross is considered a negative signal and is often interpreted as a potential indication of a downward trend or a trend reversal. Traders and investors may view the death cross as a sign to sell or take a more cautious approach to the asset.

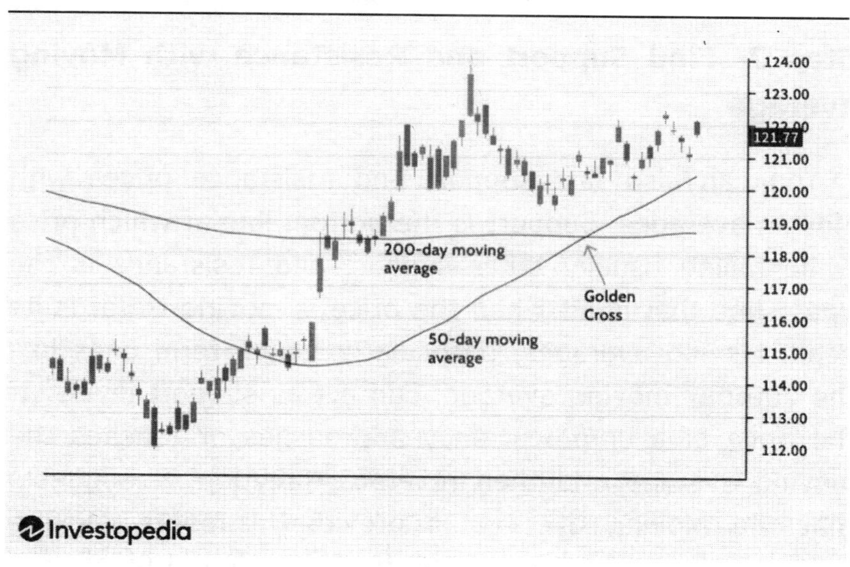

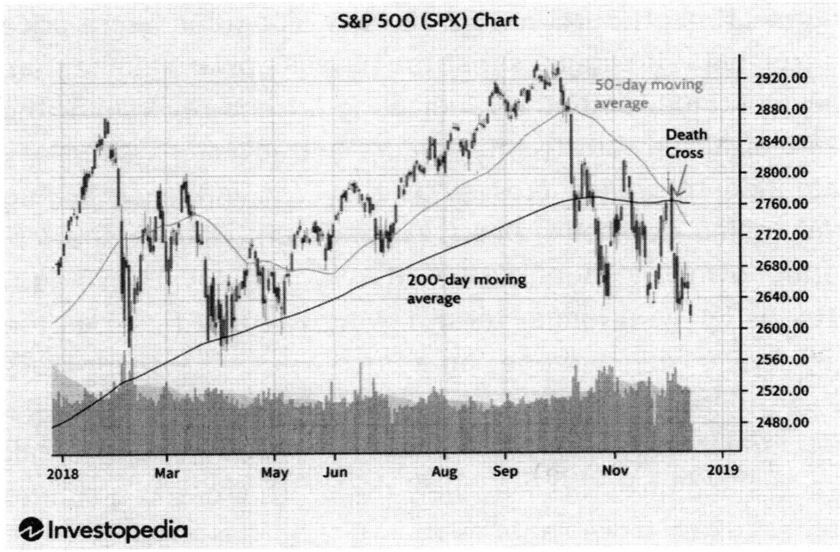

Step 7- Find Support and Resistance with Moving average

You can also find support and resistance prices with Moving averages. Support is the bottom line at which price while falling usually takes support and resistance is the upper line that is hit when the price is moving towards its peak. Moving averages, particularly longer-term ones like the 200-day moving average, can act as support levels. If the price of a cryptocurrency approaches or touches the moving average and then reverses direction, it suggests that the moving average is providing support. Moving averages, especially shorter-term ones like the 50-day moving average, can act as resistance levels. If the price of a cryptocurrency rises towards the moving average and then encounters selling pressure, causing a reversal, it indicates that the moving average is acting as resistance.

Step 8- Use volume indicator to confirm the trend established from Moving Average indicator

Using the volume indicator in conjunction with the moving average indicator can provide additional confirmation of a trend in cryptocurrency trading. Here's how it can be done:

1. Upward Trend Confirmation: When the price of a cryptocurrency is in an upward trend as you might have deciphered using moving average indicator (e.g., 50-day moving average crossing above the 200-day moving average), increasing volume can confirm the trend as it shows that there is enough market interest to support that rising price. A rising price will only sustain when the trading volume is also substantial otherwise low volume will not be able to sustain the price hike.

2. Downward Trend Confirmation: When the price of a cryptocurrency is in an downward trend as you might have deciphered using moving average indicator (e.g., 50-day moving average crossing below the 200-day moving average), volume can also play a role in confirming the trend. as it shows that there is enough market interest to support that rising price. If the volume is rising but the price is falling, it signals a strong bearish market and strong selling pressure. If the volume is lower as is the price, there is a signal of losing market sentiment and interest in the project. In a downward trend, where the price is below the moving average, volume can also play a role in confirming the trend. Traders watch for volume surges or sustained high volume during price declines to confirm the downtrend.

Step 9- Use stop loss

No matter how hard you try, to identify a perfect entry and exit point is extremely challenging especially when it comes to cryptocurrency. Since, you can't always predict the market activity, using stop loss is always important as it shields your profit against any loss. Use the explanation given in chapters above to recall, the concept, usage and types of stop loss.

Pro tip- Use trailing stop loss as it unlike simple stop loss it is dynamic in nature. It simultaneously trails in relation to the real time prices.

Chapter 12 :

My earning streams around crypto

Cryptocurrency helped me to create multiple sources of income. Some of them I thought would be helpful for my readers to read into. I have not explained them with figures and numbers for obvious reasons but I have stated the nature of the work and general outline around it. Again, a reminder, my life and my way of living doesn't mean you need to replicate the same but it may help to build a path for yourself, taking hints from the ones who are walking in the same direction. The sole purpose here of mentioning the streams is only to draw a general picture of what life of a trader and investor looks like or can look like. Alterations and calibrations according to one's own resources, interests and circumstances is suggested.

Trading : My trading over the years has evolved and has changed many different styles. At present I engage in Intraday spot trading and futures. Trading in cryptocurrency's intraday spot and futures markets gives investors the chance to actively engage in the quick digital asset markets. In intraday spot trading, trades can be immediately executed and traders can buy and sell cryptocurrencies at the current market price. Quick entry and exit from positions are possible with this kind of trading, allowing traders to profit from short-term market fluctuations. Spot traders are the ones who actually possess the cryptocurrencies, giving them the freedom to move or use them outside of the trading platform. However, the tremendous volatility present in cryptocurrency markets also affects spot trading, necessitating rigorous risk management.

- Contrarily, contracts to buy or sell cryptocurrencies at a set price at a later time are entered into in intraday futures trading. Leverage in futures trading enables traders to manage larger positions with a smaller initial investment. This increases the likelihood of losses while also boosting potential profits. Contract expiration dates must be known by traders in order to properly manage their positions. As traders must keep an eye on their margin levels and make sure they have enough cash on hand to cover potential losses, margin requirements and maintenance are critical factors in futures trading.

- Both spot and futures trading require thorough market analysis, technical expertise, and risk assessment. Traders need to stay informed about regulatory developments and be aware of the potential risks associated with cryptocurrency trading. Intraday spot trading provides immediate market exposure and the ability to react quickly to market conditions. Futures trading, with its leverage and contract structures, offers additional opportunities for profit but requires careful risk management and monitoring.

Investing: Investing is a long-term goal for me and I prefer to invest for long term in the projects as well.

- Investing in long-term trade projects that have delivered good returns can be an attractive strategy for investors seeking substantial gains over an extended period. These projects are characterized by their ability to generate consistent growth and profitability, making them appealing investment opportunities. By identifying and investing in such projects, investors can benefit from the potential for significant capital appreciation and wealth accumulation over time. Additionally, these projects often operate in industries or sectors with high growth potential, providing further opportunities for long-term value creation. However, it is crucial for investors to conduct thorough research and analysis to assess the project's financial performance, management team, competitive landscape, and market trends before committing their capital. By combining a patient, long-term investment approach with diligent due diligence, investors can increase their chances of identifying and participating in successful long-term trade projects that have the potential to deliver impressive returns.

-

- Venture Capitalist: Being a venture capitalist is a role that involves providing financial support and expertise to early-stage and high-growth companies in exchange for equity or ownership stakes. Venture capitalists play a crucial role in the entrepreneurial ecosystem by identifying promising startups and providing them with the necessary capital to fuel their growth and development. As a venture capitalist, one has the opportunity to engage with innovative founders, evaluate business models, and assess market potential. By carefully selecting and investing in promising ventures, venture capitalists aim to generate significant returns on their investments when the companies achieve successful exits, such as through initial public offerings (IPOs) or acquisitions. In addition to capital, venture capitalists often provide strategic guidance, industry connections, and mentorship to help entrepreneurs navigate the challenges of scaling their businesses. The role requires a strong understanding of market trends, industry dynamics, and a willingness to take calculated risks. Successful venture capitalists possess a keen eye for identifying disruptive ideas and the ability to support and nurture the growth of entrepreneurial ventures. It is a dynamic and rewarding role that allows individuals to actively contribute to the innovation and growth of the economy while seeking attractive financial returns. VC is typically allocated to small companies with exceptional growth potential or to those that grow quickly and appear poised to continue to expand.

- Seed Funding:As a seed investor in the crypto space, you are taking a calculated risk by investing in innovative and potentially disruptive projects that have the potential for significant returns. These projects may be developing new blockchain protocols, decentralized applications (DApps), or other crypto-related services and products. Your investment helps the project founders cover expenses such as technology development, token issuance, marketing, and community building.

- By providing seed capital, you become a key supporter of the project's vision and mission. Your financial backing allows the project team to focus on building and refining their crypto solution without the immediate pressure of raising funds. In return for your investment, you typically receive an allocation of the project's native cryptocurrency tokens or equity in the project, depending on the structure of the investment.
- Seminars & Events: I even head seminars and events sometimes. Although I do not charge tickets on my audience, the main revenue for the same comes through sponsorship.
- Blockchain consulting:A blockchain consultant helps new blockchain firms in developing growth strategies. They give advice about developing and implementing key blockchain strategies that can optimize business efficiency. Consultants begin by analyzing the effect, blockchain could have on a company and developing a plan for implementing it.
- Project marketing and Guidance: I also hold the role of a marketing advisor in some projects where a monthly fee is charged for guidance delivered by me.
- Sponsored content: A lot of youtubers/influencers earn by sponsored content on their channels. A portion of my income also comes from the same. Sponsored content needs a disclosure as per government guidelines and it is a great way to collaborate with brands and companies of your choice. I choose to only endorse

those services, products that are authentic and the ones that I can trust. Sponsored content can be in form of articles, blog, videos, audio and is a type of advertising and marketing strategy. Earlier sponsored content was very subtly placed in the storyline and was not needed to be informed to the audience. However with recent government regulations and new endorsement regulations, social media influencers must clearly identify sponsored content as such or risk paying a fine of up to Rs 10 lakh (USD 12,349) for a first offense and up to Rs 50 lakh (USD 61,746) for a second offense, or both, or receiving a six-month ban.

- Affiliate marketing: Many YouTubers include affiliate links in their video descriptions, which allow them to earn a commission on any resulting sales. Affiliate marketing is a performance-based marketing strategy in which a commission is paid to individuals or entities, known as affiliates, to promote products or services of a company. It is an advertising strategy in which the audience of the affiliate is leveraged by the paying entity to promote and popularize their own product/service.

- Subscriptions: As you know I too have a subscription model for my premium content on various channels. This is a great model to create value for your knowledge and for your skills. Subscription model connects you to that inner circle in the larger community that is ready to pay for your services. Subscription model can be a gratifying reward for that extra effort you put in and your subscribers value by paying for your hard work.

Feedback

Dear Reader,

Readers are the writer's mirror — in you, we see the reflection of our words and ideas. You help us to shape them, translate thoughts into sentences and communicate them with you.

Knowing that there are people who are genuinely interested in the ideas that we share in Twitter, YouTube and other platforms. It creates a space for conversation - writing is not a monologue.

It's an indescribable feeling to know that you've touched someone's life, maybe changed it a bit or just gave them a reminder of a thing that they've already known.

So, thank you very much!

Please give your feedback

Website: Pushpendra.info

Email: Pksjobhub@gmail.com

Twitter: @PushpendraKum

YouTube: @PushpendraSinghDigital